# THE WOOD PELLET SMOKER & GRILL
## COOKBOOK

# THE WOOD PELLET SMOKER & GRILL

## COOKBOOK

**RECIPES AND TECHNIQUES FOR THE MOST FLAVORFUL BARBECUE**

PETER JAUTAIKIS

Ulysses Press

Published by
Ulysses Press
P.O. Box 3440
Berkeley, CA 94703
www.ulyssespress.com

ISBN: 978-1-61243-559-6
Library of Congress Catalog Number 2015952142

Printed in the United States by Bang Printing
10 9 8 7 6 5 4 3

Acquisitions editor: Casie Vogel
Managing editor: Claire Chun
Editor: Lauren Harrison
Proofreader: Renee Rutledge
Front cover and interior design: what!design @ whatweb.com
Cover photo: © Brent Hofacker/shutterstock.com
Layout: Jake Flaherty
Illustration page 3: courtesy of Jeff Thiessen
Index: Sayre Van Young

Distributed by Publishers Group West

*To my wife Karen, the true love of my life*

# CONTENTS

# INTRODUCTION

Looking back, I can point to the day I fell in love with smoked meats over 20 years ago. A coworker shared some divine smoked beef ribs with me. The moist and tender ribs had a spicy sweet crust and that distinctive flavor that only an appropriate touch of smoke provides. The ribs melted in my mouth, and the flavor profiles from the rub and barbecue sauce oozed Texas-style spices. I swore then and there that I would master the art of smoking meats, but alas, I didn't follow up on that pledge. That is, until a few years later when I won a smoked pork rib roast while attending an American Legion crab feed.

My journey with smoking meats took many turns with relative success until I found my wood pellet smoker-grill. First let me say that over the years I have enjoyed great-tasting grilled and smoked meat, fish, and poultry from charcoal grills, charcoal smokers, electric smokers, wood smokers (affectionately known as stick burners), and propane grills. But I struggled to achieve the high-quality results I was striving for. After buying assorted units, I found an electric smoker that allowed me to produce smoked products to my standards. I soon joined an online forum dedicated to the electric smoker and began expanding my education on the art of smoking meats. My passion for smoked meat was fully rekindled.

As my knowledge grew I began to see the limitations of my electric smoker. Like other members on the forum, I started modifying my smoker in an attempt to broaden its capabilities. I achieved limited success. I started to hear how other wood pellet smoker-grill owners were incorporating both units. Then many owners started to abandon their electric smokers and use their wood pellet smoker-grills exclusively, not only for their smoking needs but also for roasting, baking, and grilling.

In March 2011, I joined their ranks and bought my first wood pellet smoker-grill, a MAK Grills 2 Star General. I've never looked back and now proudly wear the "Pellethead" label. You'll soon discover that family and friends will become spoiled and addicted to the scrumptious food coming off your wood pellet smoker-grill and will opt for staying home to eat rather than going out.

The techniques, recipes, and opinions expressed in this book are by no means authoritative. As you know, food is subjective, and we all have different tastes. Feel free to use the information in this book as is or, by all means, experiment and have fun.

I own a MAK Grills 2 Star General, Green Mountain Grills Davy Crockett Portable Grill, and a Traeger PTG (Portable Tabletop Grill) wood pellet smoker-grill, so all my recipes were cooked on one or more of these units.

Note: A wood pellet smoker and grill is commonly referred by some of the following terms: pellet smoker, pellet grill, and pellet smoker-grill. For the purposes of this book, we will call it a "wood pellet smoker-grill."

# WHAT IS BARBECUE?

Barbecuing is the world's oldest cooking method. My definition of barbecuing is "low-and-slow" smoking and cooking over indirect heat. The results achieved from barbecuing using smoke, indirect heat, spices, rubs, and the natural juices of meats are beyond dispute. There is a major difference between barbecuing and grilling, but many people are unaware, so they use both terms loosely. I say that grilling hamburgers, hot dogs, or chicken over some hot charcoals or a gas grill and calling it "barbecuing" is just plain wrong!

Don't get me wrong, you can barbecue great food and meals over charcoal and/or propane using indirect heat. I won't get into some of the discussions and opinions of many experts when it comes to the meaning of the term barbecue. I'll leave that up to them. Wood pellet smoker-grills are perfect units for barbecuing.

# WHAT IS A WOOD PELLET SMOKER-GRILL?

The clinical definition of a wood pellet smoker-grill is a barbecue pit that uses compressed hardwood sawdust like apple, cherry, hickory, maple, mesquite, oak, and other wood pellets to smoke, grill, roast, and bake. The wood pellet smoker-grill provides you with flavor profiles and moisture that only hardwood cooking can achieve. Depending on the manufacturer and model, grill temperatures range from 150°F to well over 600°F on many models. The days when people say you can't scar and grill on a wood pellet smoker-grill are gone!

Wood pellet smoker-grills provide succulence, convenience, and safety unmatched by charcoal or gas grills. The smoke profile is milder than other smokers you might be used to. Because of their design, they produce the versatility and benefits of a convection oven. Wood pellet smoker-grills are safe and simple to operate.

The basic components of a wood pellet smoker-grill are:

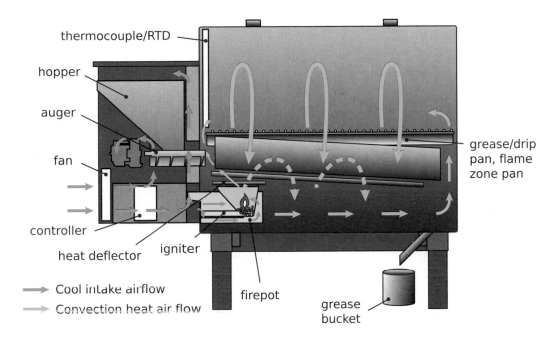

thermocouple/RTD
hopper
auger
fan
controller
heat deflector
igniter
firepot
grease/drip pan, flame zone pan
grease bucket

→ Cool intake airflow
→ Convection heat air flow

**HOPPER**—The hopper is where the wood pellets are stored. Ensure that you maintain an ample amount of pellets depending on the length of the cook, the temperature of the cook, and the hopper capacity.

**AUGER**—The pellets are then fed through the auger, the feed mechanism that delivers the pellets to the firepot.

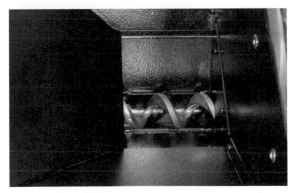

**FIREPOT**—This is where the wood pellets that heat the grill are ignited and burn. The large hole in the firepot is for the pellet tube, which houses the auger; the lower center hole below it is for the igniter rod, and the other holes are for the fan airflow. It's a good practice to empty or vacuum out the ashes after every few cooks in order to allow the igniter to work more efficiently.

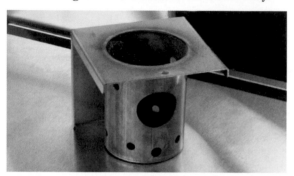

**IGNITER ELEMENT/ROD**—This rod ignites the wood pellets in the firepot. With the firepot removed you can see the igniter rod and the pellet feed tube that the auger uses to deliver pellets to the firepot.

**FAN**—The fan is very important as it maintains a variable and/or constant flow of air, keeping the pellets burning in the firepot and resulting in convection cooking.

**THERMOCOUPLE/RESISTIVE TEMPERATURE DETECTOR (RTD)**—The RTD, or thermocouple, is the thermal sensor that provides the feedback loop to the controller. The image below shows a thermocouple probe. Wipe down the thermocouple periodically for better heat measurements.

**HEAT DEFLECTOR**—The heat deflector is a specially designed plate that covers the firepot. Its purpose is to absorb the heat and spread it out evenly below the grease/drip pan, effectively turning your wood pellet smoker-grill into a wood-fired convection oven.

**GREASE/DRIP PAN**—The grease pan is used for indirect cooking, smoking, roasting, and baking. It routes the grease produced during cooking to the grease bucket. Scrape off any caked-on residue from cooks as required. If using foil (highly recommended), replace the foil every few cooks.

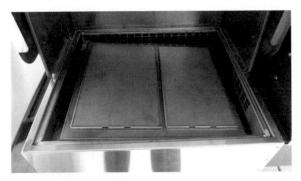

**FLAME ZONE PAN—**For direct grilling at high temperatures. Used in conjunction with searing grates and griddle accessories.

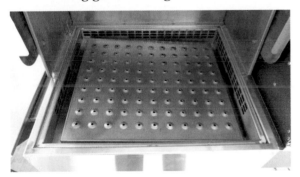

**CONTROLLER—**The controller, which comes in many forms, as you will see on page 6, adjusts the air and pellet flow to maintain the set-point temperature.

**GREASE BUCKET—**The grease bucket collects runoff grease and fat from cooking sessions. Grease accumulation depends on how much you choose to trim fat caps and excess fat from meat and poultry. Lining your grease bucket with foil helps with cleanups. I like to use an old coffee can to store my runoff grease. It's safe to dispose full coffee cans in your garbage.

# WHY A WOOD PELLET SMOKER-GRILL?

When looking for your next outdoor cooking device for your barbecue needs, your best option on the market today is a wood pellet smoker-grill. You've used the rest, now use the best! No more buying a new grill every few seasons or needing more than one grill. Wood pellet smoker-grills, allow you to smoke, cook low and slow, roast, bake, and grill, and like propane grills, they preheat in 10 to 15 minutes. With its indirect heat design there are no flare-ups, and you'll never have any of the harsh smoke flavors sometimes generated by charcoal or straight wood fires.

A wood pellet smoker-grill not only produces the best moist foods you'll ever experience, but it is by far one of the easiest to operate and maintain. Everything is automated. Merely ensure that your hopper is full of wood pellets and that your unit is plugged into a power source. The only movable parts in a wood pellet smoker-grill are the auger and fan. The tricky part to other types of smoker-grills has always been the necessary monitoring of the units to keep the temperatures steady. This is not necessary with wood pellet smoker-grills because they are designed to maintain temperatures within set guidelines.

When smoking meat, poultry, and seafood, the general consensus is that smoke is only infused into the protein when the surface temperature of the protein is below 140°F. With its extraordinary temperature control, a wood pellet smoker-grill will optimize your ability to maintain the needed lower temperatures for maximum smoke generation.

## TEMPERATURE CONTROL

It's all about control. To quote Ron Popeil on his Ronco rotisserie, "Set it, and forget it!" As we learned earlier, the controller adjusts the rate of pellet flow and the fan to maintain your set-point temperature. For the most part, most manufacturers choose a third-party controller or design their own. Obviously, not all controllers are created equal. Some are just better than others and should be a strong consideration when selecting your wood pellet smoker-grill. Look for a controller that provides pinpoint heat control. Basically there are three types of controllers: analog, digital, and PID.

**Analog controllers** are the most basic unit. They only provide three positions, known as LMH for low, medium, and high smoke. These controllers are mostly found on entry-level units. They typically do not have an RTD or thermocouple temperature probe to provide a feedback loop. This is the least desirable controller, and I would not recommend a unit with one of these. The temperature on these units wildly fluctuates and is unable to correct itself for ambient temperatures. The auger on and off durations for low, medium, and high is the only control you have and is usually set by the grill manufacturer.

**Digital controllers** use an RTD temperature probe to provide a feedback loop. Most digital controllers have a 25-degree Fahrenheit increment setting. With the installation of an RTD temperature probe, some digital controllers are a direct replacement for LMH controllers. Similar to the thermostat in your home, once you reach your preset temperature, the controller runs the auger for a certain number of seconds and then shuts off for a certain number of seconds and goes into an idle mode until the temperature deviates a preset amount. At that time the cycle is repeated. Some digital controllers allow you to adjust the idle mode to compensate for ambient temperatures.

**Proportional, integral, derivative (PID) controllers** are the most advanced controllers. They use a control loop feedback from a thermocouple temperature probe to continually compare the desired temperature with the measured temperature and adjust parameters accordingly. They allow you to set your desired cooking temperature in 5-degree increments. The PID controller adjusts the auger feed rate and, in many cases, the variable speeds of the fan to minimize temperature swings, staying within 5°F of the set temperature, and therefore, providing an extremely accurate temperature control. Most high-end wood pellet smoker-grills come with a PID-type controller, which use proprietary algorithms tuned for their units.

Many controllers, like the MAK Grills Pellet Boss digital control system, also have one or more meat temperature probe(s) and custom programming features to further enhance your cooking experience while providing total control of every aspect of your cook.

At a minimum, select a wood pellet smoker-grill that has a digital controller, and preferably, select a unit whose controller is PID-based.

# HISTORY OF WOOD PELLET SMOKER-GRILLS

Today there is a multitude of wood pellet smoker-grill manufacturers providing a wide range of excellent barbecue pits. These units cover a broad spectrum, from entry level to sophisticated pits priced from $300 to over $2,500. Just a few decades ago, this was not the case.

Wood pellet smoker-grills were first introduced in the 1990s by a small company in Oregon called Traeger Grills. Years ago I remember watching Traeger commercials featuring Terry Bradshaw, and ogling Traeger grills at my local Ace Hardware store. Those commercials made it look so simple, and I can now attest to the fact that they were right!

The industry only grew by leaps and bounds once Traeger's original patent expired. More and more people became exposed to the fabulous, mouth-watering food from a wood pellet smoker-grill, but as recently as 2008 only two companies manufactured wood pellet smoker-grills: Traeger and its rival MAK, also based in Oregon. Today there are more than 20 brands of excellent wood pellet smoker-grill manufacturers carried by a wide range of outlets from local barbecue stores, butcher shops, feed stores, hardware stores, big box stores, online outlets, and direct from the manufacturer.

# USING YOUR WOOD PELLET SMOKER-GRILL

## ASSEMBLY

You may need to assemble your wood pellet smoker-grill unless a local dealer assembles your unit for you or you buy your unit from a big box store. If you buy your unit direct from the manufacturer or an online dealer, the unit is often delivered via a ground carrier on a pallet. But don't despair; assembly is not as difficult as it looks or as hard as you might think. Just lay out all the pieces, and yes, make sure you read the instructions before you begin assembly. Tech support and assistance is only a phone call away, and most manufacturers provide outstanding customer service.

You'll find the workmanship and instructions will allow you to easily build your wood pellet smoker-grill in an hour or less. On most units you're mostly assembling the base and legs.

In no time flat you'll have your unit full of wood pellets and ready for the initial burn-in. Make sure that if and when the instructions call for two people you have someone to help you. Don't hurt yourself by trying to do it alone.

## IGNITION

Wood pellet smoker-grills require standard household 120 VAC or 12 VDC outlets to power up the ignition and operation. Some units, like the Green Mountain Grills Davy Crockett tailgate unit, for example, are designed to use 12 VDC from your car battery or a deep-cycle battery. They even provide an AC/DC converter to use with 120 VAC. The power requirements of wood pellet smoker-grills are actually quite small and are used for four items: auger, fan, igniter rod, and controller.

Wood pellet smoker-grills are very safe and simple to operate. The fire/flames are constrained within the firepot and fully covered by the grease pan, which provides indirect cooking and prevents flare-ups. When you turn on your unit, usually one of two things will happen depending on your manufacturer. Your pit either goes through a specific power-up sequence or it follows a common scenario.

The controller is turned on, the igniter rod is activated (it will glow red hot), a set amount of pellets are fed into the firepot by the auger, and the fan feeds air through several small holes into the firepot to start and maintain the fire. Depending on your controller, the igniter rod is either turned off after a set time (4 minutes or longer) or when your pit reaches a set temperature. PID controllers will turn the igniter rod back on when your temperature goes below a set temperature to prevent flame-outs.

## INITIAL BURN-IN

The burn-in procedure is used to burn off any oils and contaminants used in the manufacturing process.

Fill the hopper with hardwood barbecue-grade wood pellets. Since it may take 10 or more minutes for the auger to deliver the first pellets to the firepot, place half a handful of pellets in the firepot. Plug your unit into a grounded 120 VAC electrical outlet. Turn your grill on. If you have a digital controller, set your temperature between 350°F and 450°F, and allow the grill to run for 30 to 60 minutes at temperature (check your owner's manual for specific temperature setting and time). If your grill has an LMH controller, turn your temperature setting to high.

## SEASONING YOUR GRILL

## TESTING FOR HOT SPOTS ON YOUR WOOD PELLET SMOKER-GRILL

Not all wood pellet smoker-grills are created equal, but by learning about your grill, I guarantee that you'll be able to smoke and cook some of the greatest meals your family and friends will ever enjoy! It only takes a few practice cooks to get a working knowledge of your grill.

You'll want to test the grill surface temperatures for uniform heat and hotspots. One easy method to do this is the biscuit test. Pick up a package of refrigerator biscuits and space them in the corners, front, rear, and center of the grill. Cook the biscuits according to the directions on the package. With this test you will learn where the hotter and cooler spots are in your unit. Place and cook your food according to the information you've gained.

A more technical method requires the use of a remote temperature probe to test the temperatures in the same locations as the biscuit test. Place a remote temperature probe at each biscuit location, check the temperature, compare it to the set-point temperature on your controller, and document the temperature differences, if any. No matter how good your grill controller is, you'll find differences due to the location of the RTD/thermocouple. Just adjust your grill's set temperatures accordingly to achieve the temperatures you want.

## CLEANING YOUR WOOD PELLET SMOKER-GRILL

I recommend you keep your wood pellet smoker-grill as clean as possible. It only takes a few minutes before cooks to keep your pit clean. Cleanliness ensures your cooks are permeated with fresh and clean smoke every time. For best results, replace the foil on the grease drip pan after every long cook or after every two to four short cooks. If you choose not to use foil, then make sure to scrape off the caked residue from your drip pan often. There is nothing worse than the fumes from rancid old grease burning off at higher temperatures. After each cook, while the grill grates are still hot, use a barbecue wire brush to scrape and keep them clean. Use paper towels to wipe down both sides of the grates. I highly recommend you wear disposable rubber gloves when handling the grates and cleaning your pit.

Once your pit is fully cooled, remove the drip pan and use a shop vacuum cleaner to remove any ash from the firepot and body of the pit on a regular basis. Even though wood pellet smoker-grills are extremely efficient, you will still accumulate some ash. Large amounts of ash in the firepot can reduce the efficiency of your unit and may not allow the igniter rod to properly ignite pellets at start up. An ash buildup in the body of the pit has a chance of being blown about and deposited on your meat during a cook.

## TO FOIL OR NOT TO FOIL?

There are two camps when it comes to whether or not you should foil your drip pan. One group prefers to scrape off the burnt-on residue of cooks from the drip pan, while the other prefers to replace the dirty foil. I have always subscribed to the foil-using method. Not only does foil make it easier to clean, but I do not care to subject my meat to the fumes emitted from the burn-off of caked-on residue from previous cooks and/or old grease. When I start I prefer to have a nice, clean drip pan like the one pictured.

Here's an example showing caked on residue from smoking/cooking four pork butts. I removed one of the flame zone foiled covers from my drip pan to illustrate how much can be caked on from

Top: clean foil. Bottom: foil after several uses.

one or more cooks. For me it's easier to replace the heavy-duty aluminum foil than to continually scrape off my drip pan. I use an 18-inch-wide heavy-duty food service aluminum foil roll that can be found at most big box stores.

# WOOD PELLET SMOKER-GRILL MANUFACTURERS

Just a few years ago there were only a small handful of wood pellet smoker-grill manufacturers. Today there are over 20 and I would categorize them into three groups: entry-level, mid-level, and high-end units. I believe I would not do these manufacturers and their wood pellet smoker-grills justice were I to attempt to review their pits, because I have not had a chance to see and/or use most of the multitude of pits. I do, however, own a MAK Grills 2 Star General, a Green Mountain Grills Davy Crockett, and a Traeger PTG. I could talk extensively on the pros and cons of each unit, but that is not the intent of this cookbook.

There are excellent reviews, videos, articles, and manufacturer websites on the Internet that will better serve you in helping decide which wood pellet smoker-grill would best fit your needs. There are also forums and blogs dedicated to wood pellet smoker-grills. One excellent forum is pelletheads.com. They do not accept any advertising in order to stay neutral. One of their best features is the performance testing of pits. Manufacturers send a unit to the forum management, and usually one of two pitmasters conducts the same series of tests on every unit and posts the results from those tests for everyone to see and evaluate. Here's an alphabetical list of the wood pellet smoker-grill manufacturers that have been tested by pelletheads.com to date:

- Blaz'n Grill Works
- Camp Chef Pellet Grills
- Cookshack
- CornGlo Industries
- Dreamwerks Smokers
- England's Stove Works
- Green Mountain Grills
- Fahrenheit Technologies Inc. (Grilla)
- HomComfort
- IPT Pellet Grill
- Kuma Pellet Grills
- Louisiana Grills
- MAK Grills
- Memphis Grills
- Myron Mixon
- Ozark Mountain Pellet Grills
- Pellet Pro
- Rec Tec Grills
- Royall Wood Pellet Grills
- Smokin Brothers
- Traeger Wood Fired Grills
- WoodMaster

Not every wood pellet smoker-grill manufacturer chooses to have their units tested by the forum. This is not to disparage those manufacturers, as their units stand on their own merits.

# WOOD PELLETS

## WHAT ARE FOOD-GRADE BARBECUE WOOD PELLETS?

Food-grade barbecue wood pellets are cylindrical wood pellets about a quarter-inch wide and an inch long composed of compressed hardwood sawdust. Raw materials are sourced from whole-log saw mills or directly from orchards where fruit trees are decked up and chipped in the field. Reputable wood suppliers control the product from start to finish and guarantee there are no harmful chemicals or foreign contaminates. With the exception of vegetable oils to aid the extrusion process, the pellets contain no additives. They burn cleanly, leaving remarkably little ash.

In most cases, barbecue wood pellets are a combination of flavor and either oak or alder base wood. The percentage of each is determined by the manufacturer. Some manufacturers use a 25 percent flavor hardwood and a 75 percent base wood. Others use a 30 percent and higher flavor hardwood percentage. Certain flavors like apple, hickory, maple, and oak can be 100 percent with no base wood. Alder and oak are the most common woods used for the base wood. Today there are numerous manufacturers providing special blends, such as a base wood combined with two or more flavor woods. Due to local availability of each wood type, as a general rule, manufacturers east of the Mississippi River use oak for base wood, and Alder is used west of the Mississippi.

## WOOD PELLET STORAGE

For best results, store your barbecue wood pellets in a dry storage area like a garage or shed, on a wooden pallet if possible. If your pellets get wet or absorb moisture from being outside in the elements for a long period of time, they will eventually break down, won't perform as well, and there's a good chance they could jam your auger.

Once a bag is opened, store the remaining pellets in a wood pellet or charcoal dispenser, clean new trash can, large pet food container, plastic 5-gallon buckets with lids, or any container that is relatively air tight that will keep your pellets dry. Store the containers in your garage or a dry shed.

# WOOD PELLET FOOD PAIRINGS

Historically, protein-rich foods like meats and fish were smoked as a means of preservation. Today foods are smoked low and slow with indirect heat to impart meats and fish with rich natural flavors and produce outright delicious results. Each type of wood has its own unique flavor that suits specific types of meat. Wood pellet and food pairings are based on the smoke output on a spectrum from mild to strong. Here are the most common barbecue wood pellet flavors and their pairings:

| WOOD | CHARACTERISTICS | GOOD FOR |
| --- | --- | --- |
| ALDER | Adds a hint of mild sweetness and aroma. | salmon and other fish, beef, pork, fish, lamb, poultry |
| APPLE | The most popular and strongest of the fruitwoods provides a mild, succulent, sweet smoke. | pork, poultry, lamb, game |
| CHERRY | Slightly sweet fruity flavor. May give a rosy tint to light meats, giving a false indication that the meat is not properly cooked. | beef, pork, poultry, game |
| HICKORY | Adds a robust bacon flavor and is the most commonly used wood. | beef, pork, poultry, fish, game |
| MAPLE | Adds a tang of mild sweetness. | beef, pork, poultry |
| MESQUITE | Very distinctive, strong, spicy, tangy flavor | beef, pork, poultry, game |
| OAK | Stronger than fruit woods but milder smoke than hickory. | beef, fish |
| PECAN | Slightly spicy nutty flavor. | beef, pork, poultry |
| BLENDS | Strong, pronounced smoky flavors. | beef, pork, poultry, game |

# WHY ARE BARBECUE FOOD-GRADE WOOD PELLETS MORE EXPENSIVE?

Whether you're buying a 20-pound bag or a ton of pellets, the biggest expense is the shipping cost. Another large factor is the use of highest-grade wood components. If possible, find yourself a local dealer who stocks your preferred brand of pellets or a good variety of pellets. Spend some time trying out different brands and flavors before buying pellets in bulk. If kept cool and dry, pellets have a long shelf life. A few years ago in some areas of the country, it was extremely difficult to locally source barbecue pellets, but today, as the popularity of wood pellet smoker-grills is increasing by leaps and bounds, pellets are more readily available.

## HOW ARE PELLETS MANUFACTURED?

Pellet production starts with raw, clean premium wood feedstock in the form of sawdust, shavings, and chips. These materials are then pulverized into a uniform-size material, introduced into a large dryer drum, and dried to a desired consistent moisture level. Once dried, the materials are then transported to a hammer mill, where it is broken down to sawdust of an even smaller diameter. This fine material is then forced through a die, a metal piece with holes, with hundreds of holes 6 millimeters in diameter. The high-pressure created by the mills extruding the wood into the dies causes the temperature of the wood to increase greatly and forces the natural lignins in the wood to liquefy. When cooled, the natural lignins serve as the binding agent that holds the compressed sawdust together. Once pelletized, the pellets travel through a cooler, which substantially reduces the temperature and hardens the pellets. The cooled pellets are introduced to a shaker system, which separates any small particles and fines from the whole pellets. Fines are pieces of broken pellets and sawdust from pellet disintegration at the mill. These fines are recycled back. Finally, the pellets are introduced to an automated bagging system, where they are carefully weighed, and bagged.

## BARBECUE WOOD PELLET MANUFACTURERS

Today there are a multitude of barbecue wood pellet brands to choose from, but it's difficult to know who actually manufactures those pellets. Here is a short list—that is by no means comprehensive—of barbecue wood pellet manufacturers: CookinPellets, BBQr's Delight, Bear Mountain, Cookshack, Branch Creek Pellets, Lumber Jack, Fast Eddy's, Great Lakes Renewable Energy, and Pacific Pellet. As I said, this is not a comprehensive list and my apologies to those I have omitted.

Nowadays most wood pellet smoker-grill manufacturers carry their own pellet brand(s), but they are in the business of manufacturing grills and usually do not manufacture their pellets. The actual pellets are outsourced and manufactured to their specifications.

# ACCESSORIES

Here are some accessories that I own and use to make my cooking experiences easier and more enjoyable.

**DIGITAL MEAT THERMOMETER—**I cannot stress the importance of a good digital thermometer. I cook everything to internal temperature. Even if your wood pellet smoker-grill has one or more meat probes, get yourself a good digital meat thermometer to verify the placement of your probe(s). I use a ThermoWorks Thermapen, which reads food temperatures in 3 seconds or less.

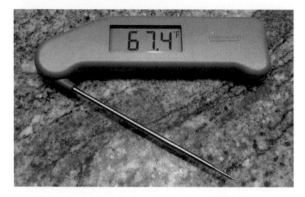

If your wood pellet smoker-grill does not have a meat probe, I suggest using a wireless remote barbecue thermometer like a Maverick ET-730 series. When you're smoking eight pork butts, it really helps to have extra probes. Care must be taken when inserting a digital instant-read thermometer or a remote barbecue thermometer to ensure you're probing the thickest parts of the meat and not touching a bone.

**SET OF KNIVES AND SCISSORS**—Make sure you have a great set of sharp knives to use on raw and cooked meats. You'll be needing your knives and scissors for trimming cuts of meat and other prep work. I recommend a 14-inch hollow-edge slicing knife for use with large cuts of cooked meat like briskets, roasts, and poultry.

**SMOKER BOX**—A smoker box allows you to cold-smoke cheese (see page 48), jerky, salmon (see page 139), meats, and nuts. It also doubles as a warming chamber to hold foods at serving temperatures. Impress your friends with some smoked Gouda and salmon. Check with your manufacturer to see if they can provide you with this capability. You won't be sorry.

**FLAME ZONE, OPEN FLAME TECHNOLOGY, DIRECT FLAME**—Many wood pellet smoker-grill manufacturers now provide the technology for direct-flame grilling. Manufacturers use different names for this technology, but the results they provide are the same. Gone are the days when you could only use your grill for indirect cooking. Now you can grill steaks (see page 80), pork chops (see page 118), meat, etc., with the best of them at temperatures exceeding 500°F.

**SEARING GRATES**—There are different types of searing grates available depending on your unit. Searing grates are designed to be used with direct flame or indirect flame technology. Check with your grill manufacturer for the type that works best with your grill. Searing grates allow you to grill your favorite cuts of meats and achieve quality that was once only found at steakhouses.

**CHICKEN LEG/WING HANGER**—Simply the best way to smoke/cook chicken legs and/or wings to perfection is with these hangers. These low-cost hangers can be found at most barbecue outlets and on the Internet. They provide increased smoke penetration by allowing the smoke and heat to circulate evenly around the chicken. As the fat drips away, it self-bastes for healthier eating.

**RIB RACK**—A rib rack allows you to cook four to eight slabs of St. Louis–style, baby back, or spare ribs at one time depending on your grill's surface area.

**TEFLON-COATED FIBERGLASS MATS—** These indirect cooking mats keep food from sticking to grill grates and allow for easy cleanup. They are FDA approved and dishwasher safe, as well. Two common brand-name products are Frogmats and Q-MATZ.

**BARBECUE INSULATED GLOVES—** I use light, flexible insulated rubber gloves to protect my hands while handling and removing food directly from the grill, and pulling hot pork butts. Simply hand-wash the gloves with mild soaps, rinse, and hang dry when you're finished using them.

**MEAT SLICER—** For precise meat slicing I use a 7-inch-blade meat slicer to eliminate the time-consuming process of slicing food by hand. For example, it works great to thinly slice tri-tip roasts for exquisite tri-tip sandwiches, or to slice smoked cheese and other meats.

**NONSTICK GRILLING TRAY—** Great for grilling, roasting, or baking items like vegetables, fish, and small or delicate foods. Cleans easily with soap and water.

**PIZZA PADDLE—** Your wood pellet smoker-grill cooks crispy, hot, delicious take-and-bake pizzas or made-from-scratch pies. To facilitate placing and removing large and small pizzas from my grill, I use a large pizza paddle rather than the provided cardboard tray. The paddles are not very expensive and they sure do work well.

**PIG TAIL FOOD FLIPPER—** This tapered shaft has a sharp, spiral snare at the tip designed to lightly pierce the edge of any food to flip or move without trouble. Use it for steaks, chops, ribs, chicken, etc.

**SILICONE COOKING BANDS—** These 2-inch bands are food- and dishwasher-safe, and heat-resistant to 600°F. You can use them to replace butcher's twine or toothpicks, and they are reusable.

**LIQUID FLAVOR INJECTOR—** This device is perfect for enhancing meat by deeply injecting marinades, flavors, brines, spices, herbs, and other products. Take care not to overshadow the natural taste of the meat.

**WI-FI CONTROLLER—** If you're a tech junkie like me, you'll want to look into Wi-Fi controllers for your unit. More manufacturers are incorporating optional Wi-Fi modules for their grills to give you full operational control of your grill remotely. I have a Wi-Fi module on my MAK Grills 2 Star General and my Green Mountain Grill, Davy Crockett. You can access your controller from your desktop, laptop, smartphone, iPad, Kindle, and/ or other tablet. As long as you have an Internet connection, you can control your pit.

Some Wi-Fi controllers like a MAK Grills Pellet Boss also have graphing capabilities to document each cook. Here is a sample of such a graph for a brisket. The green line represents the temperature that the meat probe reads, while the orange line is the temperature that the grill is set to. Note where the brisket was removed from the grill to double wrap it in foil before being returned to the grill.

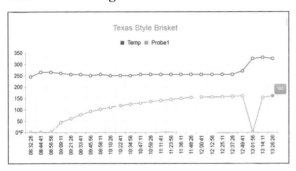

**BLUETOOTH REMOTE CONTROL**—Before the advent of Wi-Fi controllers, there were and are Bluetooth remote controllers that allow you to monitor and mimic the settings on your wood pellet smoker-grill controller. Personally, I prefer using a remote control/monitoring device than constantly going outside to check on the status of the grill or change settings.

**GRILL COVER**—Protect your wood pellet smoker-grill investment from the harshest of elements by helping to keep your grill clean and dry. I always keep my grills under a cover and covered patio when not in use.

**GRIDDLE**—Great for all facets of a scrumptious breakfast feast. Hash browns, eggs, pancakes, French toast, sausages, bacon (on the griddle or on the grates) ... you name it. Everything is always better cooked on your grill. Don't forget about vegetables and other small items.

**NOTEBOOK**—For years I have documented every cook in notebooks. It's a great planning tool for cook times, temperatures, shopping lists, sides, etc. At first glance it looks like a duplication of work, but I tweak the prep process, spices, smoke/cook temperatures, and menu items. When I get a request to cook something specific again, I don't worry because it's almost always in one of my notebooks in some form or another. Believe me when I say that at my age, I need all the help I can get with remembering.

# COOKING TIPS AND TECHNIQUES

## QUALITY MEAT AND SEASONINGS

Don't overlook your friendly neighborhood butcher shop for great and custom cuts of meats, poultry, and sausages, as well as wonderful rubs, seasonings, and barbecue sauces.

My local butcher shop, Fagundes Meat & Catering, blended their famous seasoning in 1980. Unwilling to divulge the seasoning recipe, Fagundes Meats for years chose to season their customers' meats and poultry for free. Even today, they'll still season meats and poultry for you if you ask. In 1990, butcher Frank Teixeira, the grandson of Americo Fagundes, developed Fagundes Famous Seasoning for commercial outlets after years of in-house sales and shipping the seasoning to loyal customers who left the area.

The first thing I noticed was that Fagundes Seasoning does not overpower the natural flavors of meats and poultry. The seasoning's interaction with beef, chicken, fish, pork, turkey, salads, eggs, etc., is uncanny. Originally the seasoning was only used on beef, but it quickly became apparent that it is an amazing all-purpose seasoning. The wow factor is off the charts! Knowing firsthand the combination of spices and flavors, I continue to be impressed. The seasoning really lends itself to low-and-slow cooking, smoking, grilling, roasting, frying, etc. You can purchase Fagundes Seasoning online or at some Northern California supermarkets.

I recommend you go out and explore your local butcher shops and meat markets to see if you too can find that diamond in the rough that will make your next cook an exquisite crowd-pleaser.

## FTC

A number of my recipes call for FTC resting the meat. This important acronym stands for "Foil–Towel–Cooler" and is a common method used for holding and/or resting cooked meats, such as pork butts, brisket, and turkey, in order to redistribute the juices into the meat. It produces a moist and tender finished product. Pitmasters, professionals, caterers, and restaurants use industrial units like a Cambro, for example, to achieve these results. FTC is lovingly referred to as the poor man's Cambro.

Double-wrap the cooked meat in heavy-duty aluminum foil to keep the juices contained. Wrap the foiled meat in a large towel before placing it into a cooler. If desired, minimize air space by filling the rest of the cooler with towels to help keep the heat from dissipating. FTC pork butts and briskets in a sealed cooler for a minimum of 2 hours and up to 4 to 6 hours, depending  on the meat and/or time available before serving. Take precautions when handling meat, as it will still be too hot to handle even after hours of resting.

## USDA MINIMUM INTERNAL TEMPERATURES

Cook all food to these minimum internal temperatures as measured with a digital food thermometer before removing from the heat source. You may choose to cook to higher temperatures for reasons of personal preference.

| MEAT | TEMPERATURE |
| --- | --- |
| Beef, pork, veal, and lamb (steaks, chops, roasts) | 145°F (62.8°C) and allow to rest at least 3 minutes |
| All poultry (breasts, whole birds, legs, thighs, wings, ground poultry, and stuffing) | 165°F (73.9°C) |
| Fish and shellfish | 145°F (62.8°C) |

## INDIRECT AND DIRECT GRILL SETUP

All wood pellet smoker-grills are designed primarily for indirect cooking. Indirect cooking uses deflected heat to cook more slowly and evenly. As mentioned before, the heat deflector is a stainless-steel plate that sits above the firepot. It absorbs the heat from the fire and radiates it out like a convection oven would, meaning the heat is circulated around, which gives a more even cook. Direct cooking, just as the name implies, uses direct high heat to cook. It is a faster cook time, which doesn't allow for much smoke infusion, but it can give you those classic grill marks. Today more manufacturers are beginning to provide the flexibility of a direct cooking configuration, and a small number have a built-in hybrid design providing indirect and direct cooking capability simultaneously without having to change any configuration.

**INDIRECT SETUP**—For most wood pellet smoker-grill recipes, you'll be using an indirect setup. Install your grease pan per your manufacturer's user manual. The grease pan is designed to slant in the direction of the grease bucket in order for the grease/fat to roll off. Otherwise the grease would pool on the pan and could become a flare-up safety issue at higher temperatures.

**DIRECT SETUP**—Unless your unit has built-in direct cooking capability, you may need to replace your indirect pan with a direct pan. In some units you may need to remove one or more cover plates or slide the upper portion of a combination pan to configure it for direct cooking. You slide the cover one way or the other to close or open the holes. Closed holes are for indirect cooking, while open holes are for direct cooking. Searing grates are not mandatory, but I highly recommend them. When grilling and cooking directly, they will provide greater results because they are engineered to better sear and sizzle foods by concentrating the heat.

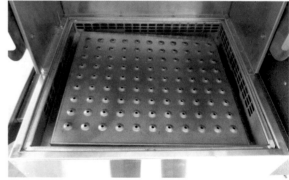

## RECIPE STRUCTURE

The recipes in this cookbook contain ingredient lists, prep instructions, and directions, accompanied by step-by-step photographs and notes, if applicable. A summary of servings, prep time, marinating time (if needed), cook time, rest time (if needed), and recommended wood pellets precedes each recipe.

**RECOMMENDED WOOD PELLET FLAVORS**—The wood pellets I recommend are just that, a recommendation. When you see multiple pellet recommendations my preferred pellet flavor for that recipe is always listed first. If you have another flavor profile you would like to accomplish, feel free to substitute it. For the most part, you can't really go wrong with anything you choose. When recipes call for "any" pellets, it just means that the dish does not get cooked for long enough at a low enough temperature to really allow for the smoked flavor to penetrate the protein, so any pellet sill suffice.

**INGREDIENTS**—Depending on how comfortable you are in the kitchen, or with the grill, feel free to substitute, remove, and/or add any ingredients based on your preferences, taste buds, and ingredients on hand. Strict adherence to the ingredients list will produce outstanding results, but don't be afraid to tweak something here and there. For the most part I have always viewed recipes as suggestions and not absolute guides. Remember that cooking should be fun.

**PREPPING FOR THE GRILL**—The prep section is all the work you do before bringing the food to the grill. The number one priority in the prep cycle is planning ahead. Give yourself plenty of time, read the recipe, and research any step or procedure you might have questions about. Recipes may call for refrigeration overnight or for hours after prepping to allow the rubs, seasonings, brines, and marinades to do their magic. Gather all necessary ingredients and cooking equipment prior to starting your prep. If not using fresh meat, poultry, or seafood, make sure that proteins are safely thawed in the refrigerator before starting. Above all, be careful to provide proper sanitary conditions.

There will be times when the prep and directions cycles can occur simultaneously. Depending on the amount of time your wood pellet smoker-grill takes to preheat, just as with a traditional indoor oven, you may choose to preheat while completing the prep.

**ON THE WOOD PELLET SMOKER-GRILL**—I recommend starting with a full pellet hopper and a clean wood pellet smoker-grill configured for indirect heat unless otherwise specified. When appropriate, insert grill meat probe(s) or remote meat probe(s) in the thickest part of the protein prior to placing the meat on the grill. Keep in mind that every wood pellet smoker-grill is different, and therefore, I provide cooking times for planning purposes only. Always rely on internal temperatures. You won't believe how scrumptious a piece of meat might look, only to find out that it's undercooked.

As you become confident with your wood pellet smoker-grill, you'll quickly learn that cooking instructions can be flexible as long as your finished product reaches the desired internal temperature. For example, you may choose to smoke a chicken for 1½ hours rather than 1 hour to provide a little extra smoke flavor before bumping the pit temperature to 375°F instead of 350°F. Overall it doesn't make any difference other than the length of the cook as long as the breast reaches an internal temperature of 165°F to 170°F.

**NOTES**—The notes at the end of the recipes contain any extra information or tips specific to that recipe. Some more general tips and techniques can be found below.

# GENERAL INFORMATION AND TIPS

**COOKING TIMES**—Cooking times in this book are given for planning purposes and can vary depending on what type of grill you have or what temperature your meat started at. Always determine the cooking time by the internal temperature reading of your food and not the cook time I have provided.

**PREHEATING**—Times for preheating your wood pellet smoker-grill may vary due to manufacturer-dependent startup procedures. The key is to run a few tests and know your grill.

**THAWING FOOD**—In order to be safe and prevent illness, always thaw food in the refrigerator; submerge it in cold water, changing the water every 30 minutes making sure the food stays submerged; or use the defrost setting in a microwave. Do not thaw your frozen food on the countertop.

**INTERNAL TEMPERATURE**—Always cook to internal temperatures preferably using a digital instant-read thermometer like a Thermapen or equivalent unit. Probe thermometers should be inserted before placing the protein on the grill and should be placed in the thickest part of the meat, not touching the bone.

**TENTING**—Most recipes call for resting the protein under a foil tent before carving or serving. Tenting is an easy technique. Fold a sheet of aluminum foil in the center, fan it open into a tent shape and loosely place it over the food. Tenting helps to retain heat while the food is redistributing its natural juices rather than releasing them on the serving plate. Skin crispness on poultry and crust on meats can be affected by tenting.

**SILVER SKIN**—Silver skin is a thin membrane with a silvery sheen that encases certain cuts of meat. If possible, it should always be removed prior to cooking. Silver skin does not break down when cooked and becomes extremely tough. To remove silver skin, slide a sharp knife, such as a boning knife, under the silver skin approximately ½ inch from the end. Then use a cutting motion, angling the blade upward as the blade moves along the base of the meat.

**THE STALL**—"The stall," also known as the "plateau" or "zone," is a natural part of the cooking process. When cooked at low temperatures, large cuts of meat reach a point where the internal temperature stops rising for a period of time. Most cuts of meat tenderize after the collagen melts and the fibers begin to separate. Every large chunk of meat like a pork butt (shoulder) or beef brisket will experience the stall. It can last minutes or as long as 4 hours, and normally occurs at internal meat temperatures from 155°F to 170°F. It's not a question of if the stall will occur, but when. You may be tempted to turn the heat up in your wood pellet smoker-grill, but exercise patience—just ride it out so as to not affect the meat being cooked.

**THE TEXAS CRUTCH—**For those who cannot wait out the stall, a technique commonly known as the "Texas crutch" will reduce your cooking time and bypass the stall. My version of the Texas crutch is to remove the meat before it reaches the full measure of the stall. I remove the meat when the internal temperature reaches 160°F and double wrap it in heavy-duty aluminum foil, making sure to leave any meat probes inserted in the meat. Wrap the foil around the probe and return the meat to the grill until it reaches your desired internal temperature.

**CARVING MEAT—**To get the most tender results, always carve meats across the grain, not with it. Identify the direction the grain is running by looking for the parallel lines running down the meat. Slice perpendicular to the lines of muscle fiber.

**PROTECT YOUR SKIN—**Wear food-grade latex-free nitrile gloves when handling raw meat and spicy peppers like jalapeños.

**KEEPING YOUR PREP SPACE CLEAN—**I prefer to line my prep area with plastic food wrap and/or heavy-duty aluminum foil. This simplifies cleanup and is also more sanitary when dealing with raw meat.

**CURING SALT—**Curing salt, which is used in some low-and-slow recipes, contains salt and nitrite and should never be used to season food at the table or in the cooking process. Large amounts can be lethal, but it's harmless in small quantities when curing meats.

**A NOTE ABOUT SMOKE—**The higher the temperature, the less smoke a wood pellet smoker-grill produces. Most units will not produce any noticeable smoke above 300°F. Therefore, use any pellets of your choice when a recipe initially calls for higher temperatures, as the pellets will not affect the flavor.

# CHAPTER 1
# APPETIZERS AND SIDES

# ATOMIC BUFFALO TURDS

Jalapeño peppers stuffed with cream cheese and topped with a Lit'l Smokies sausages are affectionately known as Atomic Buffalo Turds (ABTs). Every bite treats you to a symphony of flavor layers. If you're not a fan of jalapeños, rest assured that they get milder as you cook them. For a less spicy alternative, substitute baby bell peppers for the jalapeños.

**SERVES: 6 to 10**

| PREP TIME: | COOK TIME: | REST TIME: |
| --- | --- | --- |
| **30 to 45 minutes** | **1½ to 2 hours** | **5 minutes** |

**RECOMMENDED PELLETS: Hickory, Blend**

10 medium jalapeño peppers

8 ounces regular cream cheese at room temperature

¾ cup shredded Monterey Jack and cheddar cheese blend (optional)

1 teaspoon smoked paprika

1 teaspoon garlic powder

½ teaspoon cayenne pepper

½ teaspoon red pepper flakes (optional)

20 Lit'l Smokies sausages

10 thinly sliced bacon strips, cut in half

## PREPPING FOR THE GRILL

**1.** Put your food service gloves on, if using. Wash and slice the jalapeño peppers lengthwise. Using a spoon or paring knife, carefully remove the seeds and veins and discard them. Place the jalapeños on a vegetable grilling tray and set aside.

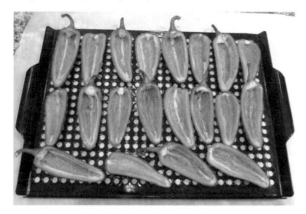

**2.** In a small bowl, mix the cream cheese, shredded cheese, if using, paprika, garlic powder, cayenne pepper, and red pepper flakes, if using, until fully incorporated.

**3.** Fill the hollowed jalapeño pepper halves with the cream cheese mixture.

**4.** Place a Lit'l Smokies sausage on top of each filled jalapeño pepper half.

**5.** Wrap half a slice of thin bacon around each jalapeño pepper half.

**6.** Use a toothpick to secure the bacon to the sausage, making sure not to pierce the pepper. Place the ABTs on a grilling tray or pan.

## ON THE WOOD PELLET SMOKER-GRILL

**1.** Configure your wood pellet smoker-grill for indirect cooking and preheat to 250°F using hickory pellets or a blend.

**2.** Smoke the jalapeño peppers at 250°F for approximately 1½ to 2 hours, until the bacon is cooked and crispy.

**3.** Remove the ABTs from the grill and let rest for 5 minutes before serving as an hors d'oeuvre.

**NOTES**

I recommend wearing food service latex-free nitrile gloves when handling the jalapeño peppers and seeds to keep the jalapeño juices from soaking into your skin.

# SMASHED POTATO CASSEROLE

Your family and friends will rave over this decadent and scrumptious yet easy-to-make potato side dish. The recipe was inspired by the "Pelletheads Potato Casserole" posted by Laurence Hill on pelletheads.com. I first used Larry's recipe a few years ago with leftover mashed potatoes from a Thanksgiving feast. The flavor profiles from the layers add new dimensions to potato casseroles. Feel free to tweak this recipe a smidge here and there as I have over the years.

**SERVES: 8**

**PREP TIME:**
**30 to 45 minutes**

**COOK TIME:**
**45 to 60 minutes**

**REST TIME:**
**10 minutes**

### RECOMMENDED PELLETS: Any

8 to 10 bacon slices

¼ cup (½ stick) salted
butter or bacon grease

1 small red onion, sliced thinly

1 small green bell pepper, sliced thinly

1 small red bell pepper, sliced thinly

1 small yellow bell pepper, sliced thinly

3 cups mashed potatoes

¾ cup sour cream

1½ teaspoons Texas Barbecue
Rub (page 171)

3 cups shredded sharp
cheddar cheese, divided

4 cups frozen hash brown potatoes

**1.** Cook the bacon in a large skillet over medium heat until crisp, about 5 minutes on each side. Set the bacon aside.

**2.** Transfer the rendered bacon grease to a glass container.

**3.** In the same large skillet, over medium heat, warm the butter or bacon grease and sauté the red onion and bell peppers until al dente. Set aside.

**4.** Spray a 9 x 11-inch casserole dish with nonstick cooking spray, and spread the mashed potatoes in the bottom of the dish.

**5.** Layer the sour cream over the mashed potatoes and season with Texas Barbecue Rub.

**6.** Layer the sautéed vegetables on top of the potatoes, retaining the butter or bacon grease in the pan.

**7.** Sprinkle with 1½ cups of the sharp cheddar cheese followed by the frozen hash brown potatoes.

**8.** Spoon the remaining butter or bacon grease from the sautéed vegetables over the hash browns and top with crumbled bacon.

**9.** Top with the remaining 1½ cups of sharp cheddar cheese and cover the casserole dish with a lid or aluminum foil.

## ON THE WOOD PELLET SMOKER-GRILL

**1.** Configure your wood pellet smoker-grill for indirect cooking and preheat to 350°F using your pellets of choice.

**2.** Bake the smashed potato casserole for 45 to 60 minutes, until the cheese is bubbling.

**3.** Let rest for 10 minutes before serving.

**NOTES**

Leftover mashed potatoes or instant mashed potatoes both work wonderfully in this recipe.

If counting calories, use fat-free sour cream, extra-virgin olive oil instead of the butter, reduced-fat cheese, and skip the bacon or use turkey bacon.

# CRABMEAT-STUFFED MUSHROOMS

Crabmeat-stuffed mushrooms are a delicious adaptation of a classic crowd favorite. These delicious bites will be the hit of any dinner party, potluck, or best of all, your own family dinner. For that extra mushroom flavor, use medium-sized portobello mushrooms.

**SERVES: 4 to 6**

**PREP TIME:**
20 minutes

**COOK TIME:**
30 to 45 minutes

**RECOMMENDED PELLETS: Any**

6 medium portobello mushrooms

extra-virgin olive oil

⅓ cup grated Parmesan cheese

**FOR THE CRABMEAT STUFFING:**

8 ounces fresh crabmeat, or canned or imitation crab meat

2 tablespoons extra-virgin olive oil

⅓ cup chopped celery

⅓ cup chopped red bell pepper

½ cup chopped green onion

½ cup Italian bread crumbs

½ cup mayonnaise

8 ounces cream cheese, at room temperature

½ teaspoon minced garlic

1 tablespoon dried parsley

½ cup grated Parmesan cheese

¼ teaspoon Old Bay seasoning

¼ teaspoon kosher salt

¼ teaspoon black pepper

## PREPPING FOR THE GRILL

**1.** Clean the mushroom caps with a damp paper towel. Cut the stems and set aside.

**2.** Remove the brown gills from the undersides of mushroom caps with a spoon and discard.

**3.** Prepare the crabmeat stuffing. If using canned crabmeat, drain, rinse, and remove any bits of shells.

**4.** Heat the olive oil in a skillet over medium-high heat. Add the celery, bell pepper, and green onion, and sauté for 5 minutes. Set aside to cool.

**5.** Gently combine the cooled sautéed vegetables with the rest of the ingredients in a large bowl.

**6.** Cover and refrigerate the crabmeat stuffing until ready to use.

**7.** Fill each mushroom cap with the crab mixture, creating a mound in the center.

**8.** Drizzle with extra-virgin olive oil, and sprinkle each stuffed mushroom cap with the Parmesan cheese. Place the stuffed mushrooms in 10 x 15-inch baking dish.

## ON THE WOOD PELLET SMOKER-GRILL

**1.** Configure your wood pellet smoker-grill for indirect heat and preheat to 375°F using any pellets.

**2.** Bake for 30 to 45 minutes, until the stuffing is hot (165°F measured with an instant-read digital thermometer) and the mushrooms are beginning to release their juices.

**NOTES:**

A mushroom is like a sponge—when washed with water it will become soft. Use a damp paper towel to clean the mushroom caps to prevent the caps from absorbing water.

Chop and add the mushroom stems when sautéing the vegetables in step 4 if desired.

Substitute the crab stuffing for shrimp stuffing (page 136).

# BACON-WRAPPED ASPARAGUS

Living in Northern California's Sacramento–San Joaquin River Delta area has given me access to all that locally grown, sweet, fresh asparagus. Every spring, for 8 to 12 weeks, the vegetable stands and grocery stores are full of it. There are so many different ways to enjoy it—deep-frying, sautéing, steaming, baking, and broiling, to name just a few—but my absolute favorite method is grilling bacon-wrapped asparagus on my wood pellet smoker-grill.

**SERVES: 4 to 6**

**PREP TIME:**
15 minutes

**COOK TIME:**
25 to 30 minutes

**RECOMMENDED PELLETS: Any**

1 pound fresh thick asparagus
(15 to 20 spears)

extra-virgin olive oil

5 slices thinly sliced bacon

1 teaspoon Pete's Western Rub
(page 169) or salt and pepper

## PREPPING FOR THE GRILL

**1.** Snap off the woody ends of asparagus and trim so they are all about the same length.

**2.** Divide the asparagus into bundles of 3 spears and spritz with olive oil. Wrap each bundle with 1 piece of bacon and then dust with the seasoning or salt and pepper to taste.

## ON THE WOOD PELLET SMOKER-GRILL

**1.** Configure your wood pellet smoker-grill for indirect cooking, placing Teflon-coated fiberglass mats on top of the grates (to prevent the asparagus from sticking to the grill grates). Preheat to 400°F using any type of pellets. The grill can be preheated while prepping the asparagus.

**2.** Grill the bacon-wrapped asparagus for 25 to 30 minutes, until the asparagus is tender and the bacon is cooked and crispy.

# BRISKET BAKED BEANS

Brisket baked beans can easily be a meal unto itself. It's a great way to use up smoked beef brisket leftovers—that is, if you have any. These beans are a wonderful complement to any meal as a side or main dish, easy and quick to assemble, and rich in sweet and spicy flavors.

**SERVES: 10 to 12**

**PREP TIME:**
20 minutes

**COOK TIME:**
1½ to 2 hours

**REST TIME:**
15 minutes

**RECOMMENDED PELLETS: Any**

2 tablespoons extra-virgin olive oil

1 large yellow onion, diced

1 medium green bell pepper, diced

1 medium red bell pepper, diced

2 to 6 jalapeño peppers, diced

3 cups chopped Texas-Style Brisket Flat (page 88)

1 (28-ounce) can baked beans, like Bush's Country Style Baked Beans

1 (28-ounce) can pork and beans

1 (14-ounce) can red kidney beans, rinsed and drained

1 cup barbecue sauce, like Sweet Baby Ray's Barbecue Sauce

½ cup packed brown sugar

3 garlic cloves, chopped

2 teaspoons ground mustard

½ teaspoon kosher salt

½ teaspoon black pepper

## PREPPING FOR THE GRILL

**1.** In a skillet over medium heat, warm the olive oil and then add the diced onion, peppers, and jalapeños. Cook until the onions are translucent, about 8 to 10 minutes, stirring occasionally.

**2.** In a 4-quart casserole dish, mix the chopped brisket, baked beans, pork and beans, kidney beans, cooked onion and peppers, barbecue sauce, brown sugar, garlic, ground mustard, salt, and black pepper.

## ON THE WOOD PELLET SMOKER-GRILL

**1.** Configure your wood pellet smoker-grill for indirect cooking and preheat to 325°F using your pellets of choice. Cook the brisket baked beans uncovered for 1½ to 2 hours, until the beans are thick and bubbly. Allow to rest for 15 minutes before serving.

### NOTES

Vary the heat factor of the beans by increasing the amount of jalapeño peppers and retaining the seeds. Pellet selection is not important at 325°F since there will be very little, if any, smoke. If desired, prior to baking the beans, smoke them for 30 to 60 minutes at 180°F to give them a smoky flavor.

# BACON CHEDDAR SLIDERS

I remember wolfing down those yummy Original White Castle Sliders back in the early '70s in Key West, Florida, while serving in the Navy. This isn't a copycat version of those sliders, but rather my homage to days gone by. These cooked-on-a-griddle, delightfully seasoned bacon and cheddar sliders are a great start to any meal.

**SERVES: 6 to 10 (1 to 2 sliders each as an appetizer)**

**PREP TIME:**
30 minutes

**COOK TIME:**
15 minutes

**RECOMMENDED PELLETS: Any**

1½ pounds ground beef (80% lean)

½ teaspoon garlic salt

½ teaspoon seasoned salt

½ teaspoon garlic powder

½ teaspoon onion powder

½ teaspoon black pepper

6 bacon slices, cut in half

½ cup mayonnaise

2 teaspoons creamy horseradish (optional)

6 (1-ounce) slices sharp cheddar cheese, cut in half (optional)

½ small red onion, thinly sliced

½ cup sliced kosher dill pickles

12 mini buns, sliced horizontally

ketchup

## PREPPING FOR THE GRILL

**1.** Combine the ground beef, garlic salt, seasoned salt, garlic powder, onion powder, and black pepper in a medium bowl.

**2.** Divide the meat mixture into 12 equal portions and shape them into small, thin, round patties (about 2 ounces each) and set aside.

**3.** Cook the bacon in a medium skillet over medium heat until crisp, about 5 to 8 minutes. Set aside.

**4.** To make the sauce, mix the mayonnaise and the horseradish, if using, in a small bowl.

## ON THE WOOD PELLET SMOKER-GRILL

**1.** Configure your wood pellet smoker-grill for direct cooking in order to use a griddle accessory. Check with your manufacturer to see if they have a griddle accessory that works with your specific wood pellet smoker-grill.

**2.** Spray the cooking surface of the griddle with cooking spray for the best nonstick results.

**3.** Preheat your wood pellet smoker-grill to 350°F using pellets of your choice. The surface of your griddle should be about 400°F.

**4.** Grill the patties 3 to 4 minutes on each side, until cooked through to an internal temperature of 160°F.

**5.** Place a slice of sharp cheddar cheese on each patty, if desired, while the patty is still on the griddle or after the patty has been removed from the griddle. Place a dollop of the mayonnaise mixture, a red onion slice, and a burger patty on the bottom half of each roll. Top with pickle slices, bacon, and ketchup.

# GARLIC PARMESAN WEDGES

Crispy on the outside, yet tender on the inside, these delectable potato wedges will more than satisfy every French fry fan. The perfect appetizer, snack, or side dish to any meal.

**SERVES: 3**

**PREP TIME:**
**15 minutes**

**COOK TIME:**
**30 to 35 minutes**

**RECOMMENDED PELLETS: Any**

3 large russet potatoes

¼ cup extra-virgin olive oil

1½ teaspoons salt

¾ teaspoon black pepper

2 teaspoons garlic powder

¾ cup grated Parmesan cheese

3 tablespoons chopped fresh cilantro or flat-leaf parsley (optional)

½ cup blue cheese or ranch dressing per serving, for dipping (optional)

## PREPPING FOR THE GRILL

**1.** Gently scrub the potatoes with cold water using a vegetable brush and allow the potatoes to dry.

**2.** Cut the potatoes lengthwise in half, then cut those halves into thirds.

**3.** Use a paper towel to wipe away all the moisture that is released when you cut the potatoes. Moisture prevents the wedges from getting crispy.

**4.** Place the potato wedges, olive oil, salt, pepper, and garlic powder in a large bowl, and toss lightly with your hands, making sure the oil and spices are distributed evenly.

**5.** Arrange the wedges in a single layer on a nonstick grilling tray/pan/basket (about 15 x 12 inches).

## ON THE WOOD PELLET SMOKER-GRILL

**1.** Configure your wood pellet smoker-grill for indirect cooking and preheat to 425°F using any type of wood pellets.

**2.** Place the grilling tray in your preheated smoker-grill and roast the potato wedges for 15 minutes before turning. Roast the potato wedges for an additional 15 to 20 minutes until potatoes are fork tender on the inside and crispy golden brown on the outside.

**3.** Sprinkle the potato wedges with Parmesan cheese and garnish with cilantro or parsley, if desired. Serve with blue cheese or ranch dressing for dipping, if desired.

# ROASTED VEGETABLES

Accentuate any main dish with these wonderful crispy, caramelized roasted fresh vegetables with delicious flavor from garlic, herbs, and olive oil. These colorful vegetables will brighten any dinner table. It doesn't get any easier than this.

**SERVES: 4**

**PREP TIME:**
**20 minutes**

**COOK TIME:**
**20 to 40 minutes**

**RECOMMENDED PELLETS: Any**

1 cup cauliflower florets

1 cup small mushrooms, halved

1 medium zucchini, sliced and halved

1 medium yellow squash, sliced and halved

1 medium red bell pepper, chopped into 1½ to 2-inch pieces

1 small red onion, chopped into 1½ to 2-inch pieces

6 ounces small baby carrots

6 medium stemmed asparagus spears, cut into 1-inch pieces

1 cup cherry or grape tomatoes

¼ cup roasted garlic–flavored extra-virgin olive oil

2 tablespoons balsamic vinegar

3 garlic cloves, minced

1 teaspoon dried thyme

1 teaspoon dried oregano

1 teaspoon garlic salt

½ teaspoon black pepper

## PREPPING FOR THE GRILL

**1.** Place the cauliflower florets, mushrooms, zucchini, yellow squash, red bell pepper, red onion, carrots, asparagus, and tomatoes into a large bowl.

**2.** Add olive oil, balsamic vinegar, garlic, thyme, oregano, garlic salt, and black pepper to the vegetables.

**3.** Gently hand toss the vegetables until they are fully coated with olive oil, herbs, and spices.

**4.** Evenly scatter the seasoned vegetables onto a nonstick grilling tray/pan/basket (about 15 x 12 inches).

## ON THE WOOD PELLET SMOKER-GRILL

**1.** Configure your wood pellet smoker-grill for indirect cooking and preheat to 425°F using any type of wood pellets.

**2.** Transfer the grilling tray to the preheated smoker-grill and roast the vegetables for 20 to 40 minutes, or until the vegetables are al dente. Serve immediately.

# TWICE-BAKED SPAGHETTI SQUASH

Spaghetti squash is a very versatile side dish. Since it's naturally low in carbohydrates, it makes a great alternative to heavy pasta and holds up well to toppings and sauces. This fun, easy, and quick baked spaghetti squash is cheesy, gooey, and just as good as twice-baked potatoes or sweet potatoes.

**SERVES: 2**

**PREP TIME:**
**15 minutes**

**COOK TIME:**
**45 to 60 minutes**

**RECOMMENDED PELLETS: Any**

1 medium spaghetti squash

1 tablespoon extra-virgin olive oil

1 teaspoon salt

½ teaspoon pepper

½ cup shredded mozzarella cheese, divided

½ cup grated Parmesan cheese, divided

## PREPPING FOR THE GRILL

**1.** Carefully cut the squash in half length-wise using a large, sharp knife. Remove the seeds and pulp of each half using a spoon.

**2.** Rub olive oil over the insides of the squash halves and sprinkle with salt and pepper.

## ON THE WOOD PELLET SMOKER-GRILL

**1.** Configure your wood pellet smoker-grill for indirect cooking and preheat to 375°F using any type of wood pellets.

**2.** Place the squash halves face-up directly on the hot grill grates.

**3.** Bake the squash for approximately 45 minutes, until the internal temperature reaches 170°F. When done, the spaghetti squash will be soft and easily pierced with a fork.

**4.** Transfer the squash to a cutting board and allow to cool for 10 minutes.

**5.** Increase the wood pellet smoker-grill temperature to 425°F.

**6.** Being careful to keep the shells intact, use a fork to rake back and forth across the squash to remove the flesh in strands. Note that the stands look like spaghetti.

**7.** Transfer the strands to a large bowl. Add half the mozzarella and Parmesan cheeses, and stir to combine.

**8.** Stuff the mixture back in the squash shell halves, and sprinkle the tops with the remaining mozzarella and Parmesan cheeses.

**9.** Bake the stuffed spaghetti squash halves for another 15 minutes at 425°F, or until the cheese starts to brown.

# APPLEWOOD-SMOKED CHEESE

Delectable smoked cheese is a great appetizer served with crackers and your favorite glass of wine. Below I have recommended some cheeses to use, but almost any hard or semi-hard cheese can be effectively cold-smoked.

Cold-smoking cheese is mostly achievable in one of two ways on a wood pellet smoker-grill. You can either use a cold-smoke box, like the Super Smoker Box accessory available for a MAK 2 Star (check with your manufacturer to see if they have a cold-smoker accessory), or a cold-smoke generator like an A-MAZE-N Pellet Tube Smoker or Smoke Daddy Cold Smoke Generator. This recipe uses the Super Smoker Box on a MAK 2 Star.

Cold-smoking occurs at smoker box temperatures between 80°F and 100°F. Smoke cheese when the ambient temperature will remain below 80°F for 2-plus hours.

**SERVES: Many**

| PREP TIME: | COLD-SMOKE TIME: | REST TIME: |
|---|---|---|
| 1 hour 15 minutes | 2 hours | 60 minutes |

**RECOMMENDED PELLETS:** Apple

1 to 2½-pound block of the following suggested cheeses:

Gouda

sharp cheddar

extra-sharp 3-year cheddar

Monterey Jack

pepper Jack

Swiss

## PREPPING FOR THE GRILL

**1.** Depending on the shape of the cheese blocks, cut the cheese blocks into manageable sizes (about 4 x 4-inch blocks) to enhance smoke penetration.

**2.** Allow the cheese to rest uncovered on the counter for 1 hour to allow a very thin skin or crust to form that acts as a barrier to heat but allows the smoke to penetrate.

## ON THE WOOD PELLET SMOKER-GRILL

**1.** Configure your wood pellet smoker-grill for indirect heat and prepare for cold-smoking by installing a cold-smoke box. Ensure smoker box louver vents are fully open to allow moisture to escape from the box.

**2.** Preheat your wood pellet smoker-grill to 180°F, or use the smoke setting if you have one, using apple pellets for a milder smoke flavor.

**3.** Place the cheese on Teflon-coated fiberglass nonstick grill mats, and cold-smoke for 2 hours.

**4.** Remove the smoked cheese and allow to cool for an hour on the counter using a cooling rack.

**5.** Vacuum-seal and label your smoked cheeses before refrigerating for a minimum of 2 weeks to allow the smoke to penetrate and for the flavor of the cheese to mellow.

**NOTES**

Soft cheese does not smoke well due to its low melting point.

Use hickory pellets if a stronger smoked flavor is desired.

Vacuumed, smoked cheese can be stored in your refrigerator for up to 6 months.

# HICKORY-SMOKED MOINK BALL SKEWERS

Traditionally, moink balls are thawed, store-bought frozen beef meatballs wrapped with bacon and secured with a toothpick. "Moink" is a combination of "moo" and "oink." This, however, is not your traditional moink recipe. I think you'll enjoy the extra "oink" my fresh approach brings to the ball.

**SERVES: 6 to 9 as an appetizer (2 to 3 balls per serving)**

**PREP TIME:**
**30 minutes**

**COOK TIME:**
**1 to 1¼ hours**

**RECOMMENDED PELLETS: Hickory**

½ pound ground beef (80% lean)

½ pound ground pork sausage

1 large egg

½ cup Italian bread crumbs

½ cup minced red onions

½ cup grated Parmesan cheese

¼ cup finely chopped parsley

¼ cup whole milk

2 garlic cloves, minced, or 1 teaspoon crushed garlic

1 teaspoon oregano

½ teaspoon kosher salt

½ teaspoon black pepper

¼ cup barbecue sauce, like Sweet Baby Ray's

½ pound thinly sliced bacon, cut in half

## PREPPING FOR THE GRILL

**1.** In a large bowl, combine the ground beef, ground pork sausage, egg, bread crumbs, onion, Parmesan cheese, parsley, milk, garlic, salt, oregano, and pepper. Do not overwork the meat.

**2.** Form 1½-ounce meatballs, approximately 1½ inches in diameter, and place on a Teflon-coated fiberglass mat.

**3.** Wrap each meatball with half a slice of thin bacon. Spear the moink balls onto 6 skewers (3 balls per skewer).

## ON THE WOOD PELLET SMOKER-GRILL

**1.** Configure your wood pellet smoker-grill for indirect cooking.

**2.** Preheat your wood pellet smoker-grill to 225°F using hickory pellets.

**3.** Smoke the moink ball skewers for 30 minutes.

**4.** Increase your pit temperature to 350°F until the meatballs' internal temperature reaches 175°F and the bacon is crispy (approximately 40 to 45 minutes).

**5.** Brush the moink balls with your favorite barbecue sauce during the last 5 minutes.

**6.** Serve the moink ball skewers while they're still hot.

**NOTES**

Use ground beef that's at least 20% fat to maximize flavor and retain moisture.

# CHAPTER 2
# POULTRY

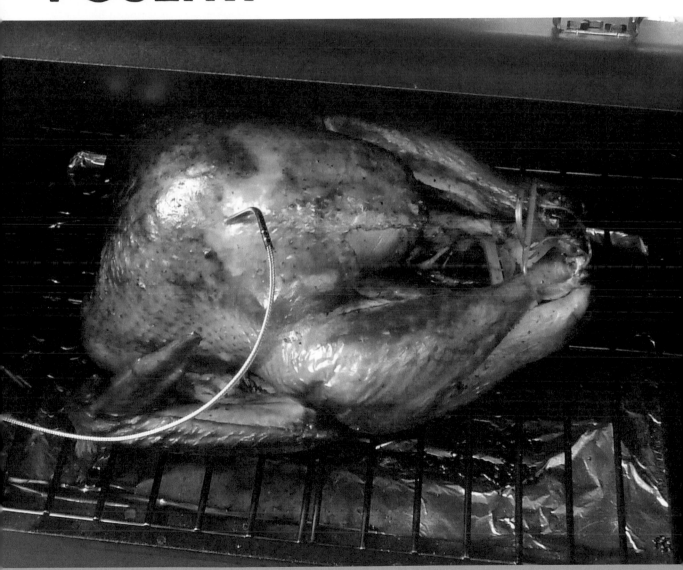

# CAJUN SPATCHCOCK CHICKEN

The fastest and best way to enjoy a juicy, delicious, smoked, roasted whole chicken is to spatchcock it. Spatchcocking, also known as butterflying, is the removal of the poultry backbone in order to press it relatively flat.

**SERVES: 4**

**PREP TIME:**
**30 minutes**
**(plus 3 hours marinating)**

**COOK TIME:**
**2½ hours**

**REST TIME:**
**15 minutes**

**RECOMMENDED PELLETS:** Hickory, Pecan, Blend

4 to 5-pound fresh or thawed frozen young chicken

4 to 6 tablespoons extra-virgin olive oil

4 tablespoons Cajun Spice Rub (page 167) or something like Lucille's Bloody Mary Mix Cajun Hot dry herb mix seasoning

## PREPPING FOR THE GRILL

**1.** Place the chicken breast-side down on a cutting board.

**2.** Using kitchen or poultry shears, cut along both sides of the backbone to remove it.

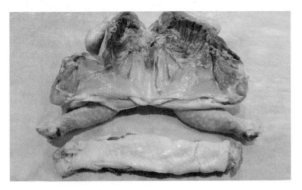

**3.** Turn the chicken over and firmly press down on the breast to flatten it. Carefully loosen the breast, thigh, and drumstick skin and peel it back.

**4.** Liberally rub the olive oil under and on the skin. Season the chicken on all sides and directly on the meat under the skin.

**5.** Wrap the chicken in plastic wrap and let it rest in the refrigerator for 3 hours to give the flavors time to absorb.

## ON THE WOOD PELLET SMOKER-GRILL

**1.** Configure your wood pellet smoker-grill for indirect cooking and preheat to 225°F using hickory, pecan pellets, or a blend.

**2.** If your unit has temperature meat probe inputs, like a MAK Grills 2 Star does, insert the probe into the thickest part of the breast.

**3.** Smoke the chicken for 1½ hours.

**4.** After 1½ hours at 225°F, increase your pit temperature to 375°F, and roast until the internal temperature at the thickest part of the breast reaches 170°F and the thighs are at least 180°F.

**5.** Rest the chicken under a loose foil tent for 15 minutes before carving.

# JAN'S GRILLED QUARTERS

Chicken quarters are economical, moist, and meaty. If you're a dark meat lover, this recipe is for you. Many recipes call for the meat to be taken to 165°F, but that's for the white chicken meat. I always take mine to 180°F. I find that dark meat is very forgiving and will still be moist and delicious at temperatures above 180°F.

**SERVES: 4**

**PREP TIME:**
**20 minutes (plus 2 to 4 hours marinating)**

**COOK TIME:**
**1 to 1½ hours**

**REST TIME:**
**15 minutes**

**RECOMMENDED PELLETS: Any**

4 fresh or thawed frozen chicken quarters

4 to 6 tablespoons extra-virgin olive oil

4 tablespoons Jan's Original Dry Rub (page 168)

## PREPPING FOR THE GRILL

**1.** Trim the chicken quarters of any excess skin and fat. Carefully peel back the chicken skin and rub the olive oil on and under the skin of each chicken quarter.

**2.** Season on and under the skins and on the backs of the chicken quarters with Jan's Original Dry Rub.

**3.** Wrap the seasoned chicken quarters in plastic wrap and refrigerate for 2 to 4 hours to give the flavors time to absorb.

## ON THE WOOD PELLET SMOKER-GRILL

**1.** Configure your wood pellet smoker-grill for indirect cooking and preheat to 325°F using any pellets

**2.** Place the chicken quarters on the grill and cook for 1 hour at 325°F.

**3.** After an hour, increase the pit temperature to 400°F to finish the chicken quarters and crisp the skins.

**4.** Pull the crispy chicken quarters off the grill when the internal temperature, at the thickest parts of the thighs and legs, reaches 180°F and the juices run clear.

**5.** Rest the grilled crispy chicken quarters under a loose foil tent for 15 minutes before serving.

**NOTES**

When resting under a foil tent, the chicken skin will lose some of its crispiness.

# ROASTED TUSCAN THIGHS

The dark meat of chicken thighs is exceptionally flavorful and succulent, and these budget-friendly cuts are easy on the wallet. For best results I always use bone-in, skin-on thighs for smoking or roasting to prevent the meat from drying out. For crispy skin in a wood pellet smoker-grill you need to roast the thighs at 350°F or higher at some point during your cook.

**SERVES: 4**

**PREP TIME:**
20 minutes (plus 1 to 2 hours marinating)

**COOK TIME:**
40 to 60 minutes

**REST TIME:**
15 minutes

**RECOMMENDED PELLETS: Any**

8 chicken thighs, bone-in and skin-on

3 tablespoons roasted garlic–flavored extra-virgin olive oil

3 teaspoons Tuscan Seasoning (page 172) or any Tuscan seasoning, per thigh

## PREPPING FOR THE GRILL

**1.** Trim any excess skin from the chicken thighs, retaining ¼ inch to allow for shrinkage.

**2.** Carefully peel back the skin and remove any large deposits of fat under the skin and on the back of the thigh.

**3.** Lightly rub the olive oil on and under the skins and the backs of the thighs. Season on and under the skins and backs of the thighs with Tuscan seasoning.

**4.** Wrap the chicken thighs in plastic wrap and refrigerate for 1 to 2 hours to give the flavors time to absorb before roasting.

## ON THE WOOD PELLET SMOKER-GRILL

**1.** Configure your wood pellet smoker-grill for indirect cooking and preheat to 375°F using any pellets.

**2.** Depending on your wood pellet smoker-grill, roast the chicken thighs for 40 to 60 minutes, until the internal temperature at the thickest part of the thighs reaches 180°F. Rest the roasted Tuscan thighs under a loose foil tent for 15 minutes before serving.

### NOTES

Chicken thighs are very forgiving and with the skin left on will retain moisture if your thighs reach higher temperatures than 180°F.

Cherry pellets provide a sweet, mild flavor to poultry but may discolor the meat in areas, giving a false indication that the meat is not properly cooked.

# TERIYAKI SMOKED DRUMSTICKS

Everyone will fight over these moist, flavorful, vibrantly colored chicken drumsticks. They are quick and easy to make too—perfect for that dark meat junky in all of us. You'll love biting through the crunchy skin to reach that succulent meat.

**SERVES: 4**

**PREP TIME:**
15 minutes (plus marinating overnight)

**COOK TIME:**
1½ to 2 hours

**REST TIME:**
15 minutes

**RECOMMENDED PELLETS: Hickory, Maple**

3 cups teriyaki marinade and cooking sauce, like Mr. Yoshida's Original Gourmet

3 teaspoons Poultry Seasoning (page 170)

1 teaspoon garlic powder

10 chicken drumsticks

## PREPPING FOR THE GRILL

**1.** In a medium bowl, mix the marinade and cooking sauce with the Poultry Seasoning and garlic powder.

**2.** Peel back the skin on the drumsticks to facilitate marinade penetration.

**3.** Place the drumsticks in a marinating pan or 1-gallon plastic sealable bag, and pour the marinade mixture over the drumsticks. Refrigerate overnight.

**4.** Rotate the chicken drumsticks in the morning.

## ON THE WOOD PELLET SMOKER-GRILL

**1.** Configure your wood pellet-smoker grill for indirect cooking.

**2.** Replace the skin over the drumsticks, and hang the drumsticks on a poultry leg-and-wing rack to drain on a cooking sheet on your counter while the grill is preheating. If you don't own a poultry leg-and-wing rack you can lightly pat the drumsticks dry with paper towels.

**3.** Preheat your wood pellet smoker-grill to 180°F using hickory or maple pellets.

**4.** Smoke the marinated chicken drumsticks for 1 hour.

**5.** After an hour, increase the pit temperature to 350°F and cook the drumsticks for an additional 30 to 45 minutes, until the thickest part of the drumsticks reach an internal temperature of 180°F.

**6.** Rest the chicken drumsticks under a loose foil tent for 15 minutes before serving.

### NOTES

Chicken drumstick dark meat is very forgiving and surprisingly retains moisture when the internal temperature surpasses 180°F. Err on the side of a higher temperature to prevent undercooked chicken.

Leg-and-wing racks are readily available at most barbecue outlets and online stores for under $15.

# SMOKED BONE-IN TURKEY BREAST

There's no need to wait for the holiday season to enjoy moist and flavorful white turkey breast meat. Bone-in turkey breasts are available year round. Smoked turkey breast will augment a Thanksgiving whole turkey or is wonderful for small crowds. Best of all, it's easy to make, great for any meal, and provides leftovers for dishes like sandwiches and casseroles.

**SERVES: 6 to 8**

**PREP TIME:**
20 minutes

**COOK TIME:**
3½ to 4¼ hours

**REST TIME:**
20 minutes

**RECOMMENDED PELLETS:** Hickory, Pecan

1 (8 to 10-pound) bone-in turkey breast

6 tablespoons extra-virgin olive oil

5 tablespoons Jan's Original
Dry Rub (page 168) or Poultry
Seasoning (page 170)

## PREPPING FOR THE GRILL

**1.** Trim away any excess fat and skin from the turkey breast.

**2.** Carefully separate the skin from the breast, leaving the skin intact. Rub the olive oil inside the breast cavity, under the skin, and on the skin.

**3.** Generously season the breast cavity, under the skin, and on the skin with the rub or seasoning.

**4.** Place the turkey breast in a V-rack for easier handling or directly on the grill grates, breast-side up.

**5.** Allow the turkey breast to rest at room temperature on your kitchen counter-top while preheating your wood pellet smoker-grill.

## ON THE WOOD PELLET SMOKER-GRILL

**1.** Configure your wood pellet smoker-grill for indirect cooking and preheat to 225°F using hickory or pecan pellets.

**2.** Smoke the bone-in turkey breast on the V-rack or directly on the grill grates at 225°F for 2 hours.

**3.** After 2 hours of hickory smoke, increase the pit temperature to 325°F. Roast until the thickest part of the turkey breast reaches an internal temperature of 170°F and the juices run clear.

**4.** Rest the hickory-smoked turkey breast under a loose foil tent for 20 minutes before carving against the grain.

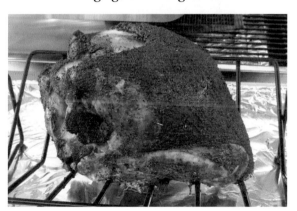

### NOTES

Using a roasting V-rack makes for better smoke/heat distribution and ease of transporting.

# HICKORY-SMOKED SPATCHCOCK TURKEY

Serving a roasted, smoke-tickled spatchcock turkey will delight your family and guests year round. It may look alien, but you'll marvel at the moist meat and crispy skin this style produces. Spatchcocking allows roasts to cook more evenly and faster than traditionally roasted turkeys.

**SERVES: 8 to 10**

**PREP TIME:**
**20 minutes**

**COOK TIME:**
**3½ to 4¼ hours**

**REST TIME:**
**20 minutes**

**RECOMMENDED PELLETS: Hickory**

1 (14-pound) fresh or thawed
frozen young turkey

¼ cup roasted garlic-flavored
extra-virgin olive oil

6 tablespoons Poultry Seasoning
(page 170) or Jan's Original
Dry Rub (page 168)

## PREPPING FOR THE GRILL

**1.** Use poultry shears or a large butcher's knife to carefully remove the turkey's backbone by cutting along both sides of it.

**2.** Flatten the spatchcocked turkey by pressing down on the breast bone.

**3.** Trim away any excess fat and skin from the breast.

**4.** Carefully separate the skin from the breast, leaving the skin intact. Rub the olive oil inside the breast cavity, under the skin, and on top of the skin.

**5.** Season the breast cavity, under the skin, and on the skin with the seasoning or dry rub.

## ON THE WOOD PELLET SMOKER-GRILL

**1.** Configure your wood pellet smoker-grill for indirect cooking and preheat to 225°F using hickory pellets.

**2.** Place the spatchcocked turkey skin-side down on a Teflon-coated fiberglass non-stick grill mat.

**3.** Smoke the turkey for 2 hours at 225°F.

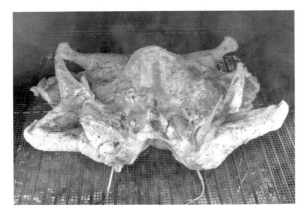

**4.** After 2 hours, increase the pit temperature to 350°F.

**5.** Roast the turkey until the thickest part of the breast reaches an internal temperature of 170°F and the juices run clear.

**6.** Rest the hickory smoked roasted turkey under a loose foil tent for 20 minutes before carving.

### NOTES

To verify accurate placement and readings of your meat probe(s), like on the MAK Grills 2 Star, I recommend using a digital instant-read thermometer to double check the breast's internal temperature. There is nothing worse or more dangerous than undercooked poultry.

# BACON CORDON BLEU

Bacon-wrapped chicken cordon bleu is not your traditional cordon bleu recipe, but I guarantee you'll enjoy my smoked-to-perfection version. What's not to like? Bacon, chicken, ham, cheese—and did I mention bacon? There's a layer of flavor in every bite.

**SERVES: 6**

**PREP TIME:**
**30 minutes**

**COOK TIME:**
**2 to 2½ hours**

**REST TIME:**
**15 minutes**

**RECOMMENDED PELLETS: Apple, Cherry**

24 bacon slices

3 large boneless, skinless chicken breasts, butterflied

3 tablespoons roasted garlic-flavored extra-virgin olive oil

3 tablespoons Jan's Original Dry Rub (page 168) or Poultry Seasoning (page 170)

12 slices black forest ham

12 slices provolone cheese

**1.** Tightly weave 4 slices of bacon together, leaving extra space on the ends. The bacon weave interlocks alternate slices of bacon and is used to wrap around the chicken cordon bleu.

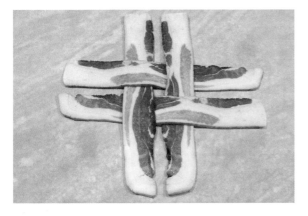

**2.** Spritz or rub 2 thin chicken breast fillets with the olive oil on both sides.

**3.** Dust both sides of the chicken breast fillets with the seasoning.

**4.** Layer one seasoned chicken fillet on the bacon weave and top with 1 slice each of ham and provolone cheese.

**5.** Repeat the process with another chicken fillet, ham, and cheese. Fold the chicken, ham, and cheese in half.

**6.** Overlap the bacon strips from opposite corners to completely cover the chicken cordon blue.

**7.** Use silicone food-grade cooking bands, butcher's twine, or toothpicks to secure the bacon strips in place.

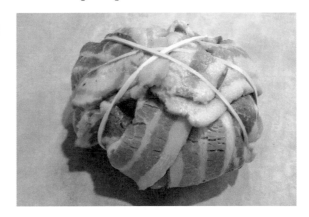

**8.** Repeat the process for the remaining chicken breasts and ingredients.

## ON THE WOOD PELLET SMOKER-GRILL

**1.** Configure your wood pellet smoker-grill for indirect cooking and preheat for smoking (180°F to 200°F) using apple or cherry pellets.

**2.** Smoke the bacon cordon bleu for 1 hour.

**3.** After smoking for an hour, increase the pit temperature to 350°F.

**4.** The bacon cordon bleu is done when the internal temperature reaches 165°F and the bacon is crisp.

**5.** Rest under a loose foil tent for 15 minutes before serving.

**NOTES**

My local Latin American butcher shop took three large chicken breasts and provided me with six double-wide thin slices, which I split into 12 chicken fillets. The butcher's butterfly technique was a work of art. If you live close to or know a good butcher, ask them to slice your chicken breasts for you.

# CRAB-STUFFED LEMON CORNISH HENS

This surf-and-turf recipe will delight seafood and chicken lovers. There's a lot to be said for having your own little chicken in one sitting. A Cornish hen simply refers to a chicken that's about five weeks old. Ever since my family and I enjoyed a Cornish hen, without utensils, at a medieval show, they've always been a special treat for us, and the crabmeat stuffing takes them over the top.

**SERVES: 2 to 4**

**PREP TIME:**
30 minutes (plus 2 to 3 hours marinating)

**COOK TIME:**
1½ hours

**REST TIME:**
15 minutes

**RECOMMENDED PELLETS: Any**

2 Cornish hens (about 1¾ pounds each)

1 lemon, halved

4 tablespoons Pete's Western Rub (page 169) or any poultry rub

2 cups Crabmeat Stuffing (page 34)

## PREPPING FOR THE GRILL

**1.** Thoroughly rinse the hens inside and out and pat dry.

**2.** Carefully loosen the breast and leg skin. Rub the lemon under and on the skin and inside the cavity. Rub the Pete's Western Rub under and on the breast and leg skin. Carefully return the skin to its original position.

**3.** Wrap the Cornish hens in plastic wrap and refrigerate for 2 to 3 hours to give the flavors time to absorb.

**4.** Prepare the Crabmeat Stuffing according to the directions. Be sure it has fully cooled before stuffing the hens. Loosely stuff each hen cavity with the crab stuffing.

**5.** Tie the Cornish hen legs together with butcher's twine to keep the stuffing in.

## ON THE WOOD PELLET SMOKER-GRILL

**1.** Configure your wood pellet smoker-grill for indirect cooking and preheat to 375°F with any pellets.

**2.** Place the stuffed hens on a rack inside a baking dish. You can also place the hens directly in the baking dish if you don't have a rack small enough to fit.

**3.** Roast the hens at 375°F until the internal temperature, at the thickest part of the breast, reaches 170°F, the thighs reach 180°F, and the juices run clear.

**4.** Test the crabmeat stuffing to see if it has reached a temperature of 165°F.

**5.** Rest the roasted hens under a loose foil tent for 15 minutes before serving.

**NOTES**

Cornish hens should never be stuffed in advance and refrigerated, as it may increase the risk of bacteria growth. Stuff them right before cooking.

When poultry is stuffed, the cooking times will increase.

# CURED TURKEY DRUMSTICKS

Now you can enjoy delicious monster smoked turkey legs that you normally find at amusement parks, and county and state fairs, in your own backyard. Curing salt gives turkey drumsticks a slight ham flavor and a pink color to the meat when smoked.

**SERVES: 3**

**PREP TIME:**
**20 minutes (plus 14 hours brining/drying)**

**COOK TIME:**
**2½ to 3 hours**

**REST TIME:**
**15 minutes**

**RECOMMENDED PELLETS: Hickory, Maple**

3 large fresh or thawed frozen turkey drumsticks

3 tablespoons extra-virgin olive oil

**BRINE INGREDIENTS**

4 cups filtered water

¼ cup kosher salt

¼ cup brown sugar

1 teaspoon garlic powder

1 teaspoon Poultry Seasoning (page 170)

½ teaspoon red pepper flakes

⅛ teaspoon pink curing salt #1 (see note)

## PREPPING FOR THE GRILL

**1.** Combine the brine ingredients in a 1-gallon sealable bag. Add the turkey drumsticks to the brine and refrigerate for 12 hours.

**2.** After 12 hours, remove the drumsticks from the brine, rinse them with cool water, and pat them dry with a paper towel.

**3.** Allow the drumsticks to air-dry, uncovered, in the refrigerator for 2 hours.

**4.** Remove the drumsticks from refrigerator and rub 1 tablespoon extra-virgin olive oil under and on the skin of each drumstick.

## ON THE WOOD PELLET SMOKER-GRILL

**1.** Configure your wood pellet smoker-grill for indirect cooking and preheat to 250°F using hickory or maple pellets.

**2.** Place the drumsticks on the grill grates and smoke them at 250°F for 2 hours.

**3.** After 2 hours, increase the grill temperature to 325°F.

**4.** Cook the turkey drumsticks at 325°F until the internal temperature at the thickest part of each drumstick measures 180°F with an instant-read digital thermometer.

**5.** Rest the smoked turkey drumsticks under a loose foil tent for 15 minutes before serving.

### NOTES

Curing salt contains salt and nitrite and should never be used to season food at the table or in the cooking process. Most curing salts are colored pink to prevent confusing them with table salt. Extreme care must be taken when using pink curing salt #1, also called Prague powder #1. Large amounts can be lethal, but it's harmless in small quantities when curing meats. Pink curing salt #1 can be found at butcher shops and online.

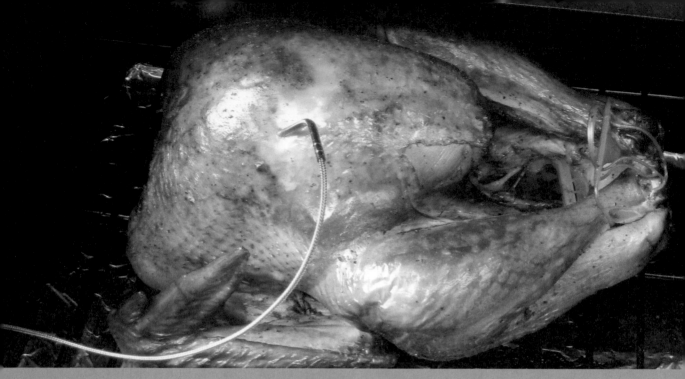

# TAILGATE SMOKED YOUNG TURKEY

During the holiday season you can find fresh young turkeys at most stores and butcher shops. They are perfect for intimate gatherings or a small family feast with all the trimmings. But don't limit yourself to the holidays—enjoy a smoked turkey year round. It doesn't get any better than smoked turkey! This recipe uses a Green Mountain Grills portable Davy Crockett wood pellet smoker-grill, which is perfect for tailgating, camping, or at-home use. This recipe works equally well with any grill.

**SERVES: 8 to 10**

| PREP TIME: | COOK TIME: | REST TIME: |
|---|---|---|
| **20 minutes** | **4 to 4½ hours** | **20 minutes** |

**RECOMMENDED PELLETS: Apple, Cherry**

1 (10-pound) fresh or thawed frozen young turkey

6 tablespoons roasted garlic-flavored extra-virgin olive oil

6 tablespoons Jan's Original Dry Rub (page 168) or Poultry Seasoning (page 170)

## PREPPING FOR THE GRILL

**1.** Trim away any excess fat and skin from the breast and cavity of the turkey.

**2.** Carefully separate the skin from turkey breast and leg quarters, leaving the skin intact.

**3.** Rub the olive oil inside the breast cavity, under the skin, and on the skin.

**4.** Generously season the breast cavity, under the skin, and on the skin with the rub or seasoning.

## ON THE WOOD PELLET SMOKER-GRILL

**1.** Configure your tailgate wood pellet smoker-grill for indirect cooking and smoking. Preheat to 225°F using apple or cherry pellets.

**2.** Place the turkey, breast-side up, on the grill.

**3.** Smoke the turkey for 4 to 4½ hours at 225°F until the thickest part of the turkey breast reaches an internal temperature of 170°F and the juices run clear.

**4.** Rest the turkey under a loose foil tent for 20 minutes before carving.

# ROASTED DUCK À L'ORANGE

Fit for any festive occasion, a roasted whole duck à l'orange will delight and impress anyone. More majestic than turkey and more elegant than chicken, roasting a whole duck is not as difficult as you may have been led to believe. Experience a world of intense flavor that you won't find with a traditional chicken recipe.

**SERVES: 3 to 4**

| PREP TIME: | COOK TIME: | REST TIME: |
|---|---|---|
| 30 minutes | 2 to 2½ hours | 20 minutes |

**RECOMMENDED PELLETS: Any**

1 (5 to 6-pound) frozen Long Island, Peking, or Canadian duck

3 tablespoons Pete's Western Rub (page 169) or Poultry Seasoning (page 170), divided

1 large orange, cut into wedges

3 celery stalks, chopped into large chunks

½ small red onion, quartered

**FOR THE ORANGE SAUCE:**

2 cups orange juice

2 tablespoons soy sauce

2 tablespoons orange marmalade

2 tablespoons honey

3 teaspoons grated fresh ginger

## PREPPING FOR THE GRILL

**1.** Remove any giblets from cavity and neck of the duck and retain for another use or discard. Rinse the duck and pat it dry with a paper towel.

**2.** Trim any excess fat from the tail, neck, and cavity area. Making sure not to penetrate the duck meat, use the tip of a sharp paring knife to prick the duck skin all over to facilitate melting the fat layer under the skin.

**3.** Season the inside of the cavity with 1 tablespoon of the rub or seasoning.

**4.** Season the outside of the duck with the remaining rub or seasoning.

**5.** Stuff orange wedges, celery, and onion into the cavity. Tie the duck legs together with butcher's twine to help keep the stuffing in. Place the duck breast-side up on a small rack in a shallow roasting pan.

**6.** To make the sauce, combine the ingredients in a saucepan over low heat and simmer until the sauce thickens and is syrupy. Set aside and allow to cool.

**1.** Configure your wood pellet smoker-grill for indirect cooking and preheat to 350°F using any pellets.

**2.** Roast the duck at 350°F for 2 hours.

**3.** After 2 hours, brush the duck liberally with the orange sauce.

**4.** Roast the orange-glazed duck for an additional 30 minutes and verify that the internal temperature, at the thickest part of the legs, reaches 165°F.

**5.** Rest the duck under a loose foil tent for 20 minutes before serving.

**6.** Discard the orange wedges, celery, and onion. Quarter the duck with poultry shears and serve.

**NOTES**

Thaw frozen duck in the refrigerator for 48 hours.

Some ducks come packaged with orange sauce. If you would like, use the provided orange sauce instead of the orange sauce recipe above.

# CHAPTER 3
# RED MEAT

# PERFECTLY GRILLED STEAKS

New York strip steaks, with their beautiful marbling, strong beefy flavor, and perfect tenderness, are a favorite at steakhouses. Elevate any meal to a magnificent occasion by grilling the perfect New York strip steak at home. In this recipe I call for 1¼ to 1½-inch-thick steaks—the thickness of the steak is more important than the weight here.

**SERVES: 2**

**PREP TIME:**
60 minutes

**COOK TIME:**
15 minutes

**REST TIME:**
5 minutes

**RECOMMENDED PELLETS: Any**

2 USDA Choice or Prime 1¼ to 1½-inch-thick New York strip steaks (about 12 to 14 ounces each)

extra-virgin olive oil

4 teaspoons Pete's Western Rub (page 169) or salt and pepper, divided

## PREPPING FOR THE GRILL

**1.** Remove the steaks from the refrigerator and cover loosely with plastic wrap about 45 minutes before cooking to bring them to room temperature.

**2.** Once the steaks reach room temperature, brush them on both sides with olive oil.

**3.** Season each side of the steaks with 1 teaspoon of the rub or salt and pepper, and then let stand at room temperature for at least 5 minutes before grilling.

## ON THE WOOD PELLET SMOKER-GRILL

**1.** Configure your wood pellet smoker-grill for direct cooking by using searing grates (page 17), set the temperature to high, and preheat to at least 450°F using any pellets.

**2.** Place the steaks on the grill and cook on one side until slightly charred, 2 to 3 minutes.

**3.** On the same side, rotate the steaks 90 degrees for cross grill marks, and cook for an additional 2 to 3 minutes.

**4.** Flip the steaks over and grill until they reach desired doneness:

- 3 to 5 minutes for medium rare (an internal temperature of 135°F)
- 6 to 7 minutes for medium (an internal temperature of 140°F)
- 8 to 10 minutes for medium-well (an internal temperature of 150°F)

**5.** Transfer the steaks to a platter, tent loosely with foil, and let rest 5 minutes before serving.

**NOTES**

When still attached to the bone, the strip steak is known as a T-bone, porterhouse, or sometimes, a Kansas City steak.

To prevent juices from escaping, avoid piercing your steaks during cooking.

I recommend using a pig tail food flipper to rotate and flip the meat rather than tongs.

To add extra flavor and moisture to your New York strip steak during cooking, don't trim the fat off.

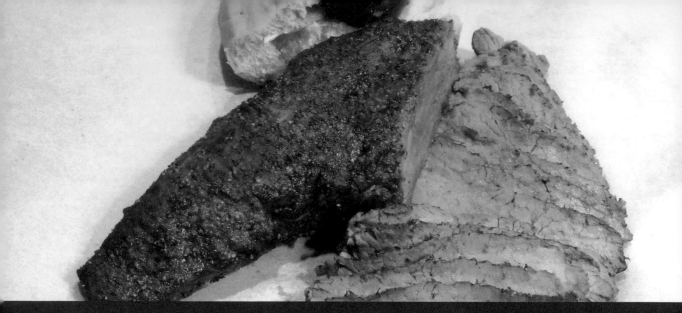

# SMOKED TRI-TIP ROAST

Tri-tip roasts have long been a delicacy in the Central Coast and San Joaquin Valley of California. Until recently, most of the country had never heard of this triangular-shaped cut from the bottom of the sirloin primal. Historically, the tri-tip was cut up for stew meat or ground into hamburger.

In the 1950s, Bob Schutz, a butcher and meat manager of a Safeway market in Santa Maria, California, had plenty of stew meat and hamburger, so he decided to barbecue the tri-tip over locally available red oak wood. The rest, as they say, is history!

**SERVES: 4 to 6**

**PREP TIME:**
20 minutes (plus overnight marinating)

**COOK TIME:**
2 hours

**REST TIME:**
15 minutes

**RECOMMENDED PELLETS: Hickory, Blend**

1 (2½ to 3-pound) whole peeled tri-tip roast

3 tablespoons roasted garlic-flavored extra-virgin olive oil

3 tablespoons Pete's Western Rub (page 169) or your favorite Santa Maria–style rub

## PREPPING FOR THE GRILL

**1.** Rub all sides of the tri-tip with the olive oil and then with the Pete's Western Rub or other rub.

**2.** Double-wrap the seasoned tri-tip roast with plastic wrap and refrigerate overnight.

## ON THE WOOD PELLET SMOKER-GRILL

**1.** Configure your wood pellet smoker-grill for indirect heat and preheat to 180°F using hickory pellets or a blend.

**2.** If your unit has one, insert your wood pellet smoker-grill meat probe into the thickest part of the tri-tip roast and smoke for 1 hour.

**3.** After an hour, increase the pit temperature to 325°F. Cook until the internal temperature reaches 140° to 145°F.

**4.** Rest the smoked tri-tip under a loose foil tent for 15 minutes before serving.

**5.** Slice the roast against the grain using the illustration below as a guide.

**NOTES**

Peeled tri-tip roasts are those that have their fat cap and silver skin removed by the butcher.

The grains of a tri-tip roast run in different directions as you can see in the image below.

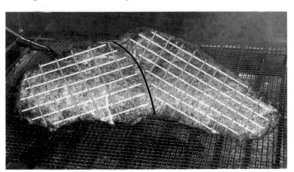

Black line: Seam of fat down the center of tri-tip roast.

White lines: Direction of the grains; note how grains are different on each side of the black line.

Blue lines: Carving direction.

Cut the tri-tip in half along the black line. Carve along the blue lines on the bias at a 45-degree angle.

# MEATY CHUCK SHORT RIBS

Smoked low and slow, beef chuck short ribs are juicy and melt-in-your-mouth tender, and the flavor profiles will rival any beef brisket. The big, marbled ribs will delight any dinner table.

**SERVES: 2 to 4**

**PREP TIME:**
20 minutes

**COOK TIME:**
5 to 6 hours

**REST TIME:**
15 minutes

**RECOMMENDED PELLETS: Mesquite, Hickory**

English-cut 4-bone slab beef chuck short ribs

3 to 4 tablespoons yellow mustard or extra-virgin olive oil

3 to 5 tablespoons Pete's Western Rub (page 169)

## PREPPING FOR THE GRILL

**1.** Trim the fat cap from the ribs, leaving a ¼ inch fat, and remove any silver skin.

**2.** Remove the membrane from the bones to season the meat properly by working a spoon handle under the membrane to get

a piece lifted. Use a paper towel to grab the membrane and pull it off the bones.

**3.** Slather the mustard or olive oil on all sides of the short rib slab. Season liberally on all sides with the rub.

## ON THE WOOD PELLET SMOKER-GRILL

**1.** Configure your wood pellet smoker-grill for indirect heat and preheat to 225°F using mesquite or hickory pellets.

**2.** Insert your wood pellet smoker-grill or a remote meat probe into the thickest part of the slab of ribs. If your grill does not have meat probe capabilities or you don't own a remote meat probe, then use an instant-read digital thermometer during the cook for internal temperature readings.

**3.** Place the short ribs bone-side down on the grill and smoke at 225°F for 5 hours.

**4.** If after 5 hours the ribs have not reached an internal temperature of at least 195°F, then increase the pit temperature to 250°F until the internal temperature reaches 195° to 205°F.

**5.** Rest the smoked short ribs under a loose foil tent for 15 minutes before serving.

**NOTES**

Surprisingly, common yellow mustard, used as a glue for your rub or seasoning, does not give the meat a mustard flavor.

# HICKORY NEW YORK STRIP ROAST

Smoked low and slow to medium-rare, a New York strip roast is delicious and tender. It's elegant enough for any special occasion and reasonably priced to grace your dinner table any day of the week. Enjoy leftovers in salads or succulent sandwiches.

**SERVES: 6 to 8**

| PREP TIME: | COOK TIME: | REST TIME: |
|---|---|---|
| 30 minutes (plus overnight marinating and rest time) | 2½ to 3 hours | 20 minutes |

**RECOMMENDED PELLETS: Hickory**

1 (6-pound) beef New York strip roast, USDA Choice or Prime grade

¼ cup roasted garlic-flavored extra-virgin olive oil

¼ cup Texas Barbecue Rub (page 171) or your favorite prime rib seasoning

## PREPPING FOR THE GRILL

**1.** Use a sharp boning knife to remove the fat cap from the roast and trim away any additional excess fat and silver skin.

**2.** Rub all sides of the roast with the olive oil, and liberally season on all sides with the rub or seasoning.

**3.** Double-wrap the seasoned roast with plastic wrap and refrigerate overnight.

## ON THE WOOD PELLET SMOKER-GRILL

**1.** Remove the roast from the refrigerator 45 minutes prior to cooking to allow it to come to room temperature.

**2.** Configure your wood pellet smoker-grill for indirect cooking and preheat to 240°F using hickory pellets.

**3.** Insert your wood pellet smoker-grill meat probe or a remote meat thermometer into the thickest part of the roast. Smoke the New York strip roast at 240°F for approximately 2½ to 3 hours.

**4.** Remove the smoked roast when the internal temperature reaches 135°F.

**5.** Rest the roast under a loose foil tent for 20 minutes before serving. Slice the roast against the grain to the desired thickness.

# TEXAS-STYLE BRISKET FLAT

Brisket is one of the most universally loved cuts of beef. It comes from the breast or lower chest of the steer. As one of the toughest cuts of beef, a brisket is ideal for low-and-slow cooking on a wood pellet smoker-grill. A 6 to 8-pound brisket flat should only take about 5½ hours to reach an internal temperature of 205°F if you use a technique commonly known as the "Texas crutch" to reduce your cooking time. This technique entails double-wrapping the brisket tightly in heavy-duty aluminum foil to bypass the stall and tenderize the meat. Couple the Texas crutch with resting the brisket for 2 to 4 hours using the FTC method (page 20), and you'll no longer have to fear briskets. So don't let traditional cooking times and the size of a brisket deter you. Jump in—your guests will love you for it and wolf this brisket down.

**SERVES: 8 to 10**

**PREP TIME:**
**45 minutes (plus overnight marinating, optional)**

**COOK TIME:**
**5 to 6 hours**

**REST TIME:**
**2 to 4 hours**

**RECOMMENDED PELLETS: Mesquite, Oak**

6½ pound beef brisket flat

½ cup roasted garlic–flavored extra-virgin olive oil

½ cup Texas-Style Brisket Rub (page 171) or your favorite brisket rub

## PREPPING FOR THE GRILL

**1.** Trim the fat cap off of the brisket and remove any silver skin.

**2.** Rub the trimmed meat on all sides with the olive oil.

**3.** Apply the rub to all sides of the brisket, ensuring that it is completely covered with the rub.

**4.** Double-wrap the brisket in plastic wrap and refrigerate overnight for the rub to penetrate the meat or, if you prefer, you can cook the brisket immediately.

## ON THE WOOD PELLET SMOKER-GRILL

**1.** Remove the brisket from the refrigerator and insert your wood pellet smoker-grill or a remote meat probe into the thickest part of the meat. If your grill does not have meat probe, capabilities or you don't own a remote meat probe, then use an instant-read digital thermometer during the cook for internal temperature readings.

**3.** Smoke the brisket at 250°F, until the internal temperature reaches 160°F (about 4 hours).

**2.** Configure your wood pellet smoker-grill for indirect cooking and preheat to 250°F using mesquite or oak pellets.

**4.** Remove the brisket from the grill, double-wrap it in heavy-duty aluminum foil, making sure to keep the meat probe in place, and return it to the smoker-grill.

**5.** Increase the pit temperature to 325°F, and cook the brisket until the internal temperature reaches 205°F, about another 2 hours.

**6.** Remove the foiled brisket, wrap it in a towel, and place it in cooler, referring to the FTC instructions on page 20. Let sit in the cooler for 2 to 4 hours before slicing against the grain and serving.

**NOTES**

The "stall" is inevitable when smoking large portions of meat like brisket, pork butt, or turkey. Don't be tempted to increase the pit temperature when your internal temperature remains the same, sometimes for hours.

# PETE-ZZA MEATLOAF

The ultimate comfort food has to be meatloaf, in my humble opinion. But I really love pizza too. Now you can enjoy the best of all worlds: a smoked meatloaf stuffed with pizza ingredients. Your family and friends will inhale this loaf. From the smoke ring to the vivid colors of the stuffing, this recipe makes a stunning presentation and will tickle your taste buds beyond expectations.

**SERVES: 6 to 8**

| PREP TIME: | COOK TIME: | REST TIME: |
|---|---|---|
| 30 to 45 minutes | 2 to 2½ hours | 15 minutes |

**RECOMMENDED PELLETS: Oak, Blend**

**FOR THE MEATLOAF:**

1 pound 80% lean ground beef

1 pound pork sausage, like Jimmy Dean

2 large eggs

1 cup Italian bread crumbs

½ cup pizza sauce, plus an additional ½ cup, to serve

½ teaspoon garlic salt

½ teaspoon seasoned salt

½ teaspoon ground pepper

½ teaspoon granulated garlic

**FOR THE PIZZA STUFFING:**

2 tablespoons extra-virgin olive oil

1 cup sliced portobello mushrooms
(about 6 small mushrooms)

⅔ cup sliced red onion (1 small onion)

⅔ cup sliced green bell pepper
(1 medium green pepper)

½ cup sliced red bell pepper
(1 small red pepper)

pinch of salt and black pepper

2 cups shredded mozzarella cheese

2 cups shredded cheddar or Jack cheese

3 ounces sliced pepperoni sausage

## PREPPING FOR THE GRILL

**1.** In a large bowl, combine the meatloaf ingredients thoroughly using your hands for best results.

**2.** In a medium skillet, heat the olive oil over medium-high heat and sauté the mushrooms, red onion, green bell pepper, and red bell pepper for about 2 minutes, until the vegetables are al dente. Season the vegetables with a pinch of salt and black pepper. Set aside.

**3.** On parchment paper, flatten the meatloaf into a ⅜-inch-thick rectangle. Evenly spread the sautéed vegetables over the meat. Top the vegetables with the mozzarella, followed by the cheddar or Jack. Top the cheese with the pepperoni.

**4.** Use the parchment paper to roll the meatloaf, making sure to seal the ends and all seams.

## ON THE WOOD PELLET SMOKER-GRILL

**1.** Configure your wood pellet-smoker grill for indirect heat and preheat to 225°F using oak pellets or a blend.

**2.** Smoke the stuffed pizza meatloaf for 1 hour.

**3.** After an hour, increase the pit temperature to 350°F, and cook until the internal temperature of the stuffed pizza meatloaf reaches 170°F.

**4.** Top the meatloaf with the remaining ½ cup pizza sauce and let rest under a loose foiled tent for 15 minutes before serving.

### NOTES

If your wood pellet smoker-grill does not have a built-in meat probe, you'll want to use a digital instant-read thermometer to verify your meatloaf internal temperature.

# TRAFFIC LIGHT STUFFED BELL PEPPERS

Who says you can only use one color of pepper for a dish? The vibrant colors of these smoked stuffed bell peppers will delight your family and friends. Make sure to cook plenty and watch people fight over their favorite color.

You never know where you'll get your inspiration for a recipe. I got mine while waiting at a traffic light. Red light, green light, and no—yellow does not mean accelerate!

**SERVES: 4 to 6**

**PREP TIME:**
30 to 45 minutes

**COOK TIME:**
90 minutes

**REST TIME:**
10 minutes

**RECOMMENDED PELLETS: Apple, Hickory**

6 to 8 large bell peppers
(green, yellow, and red)

1 small red onion

3 celery stalks

2 tablespoons extra-virgin olive oil

1 pound 80% lean ground beef

1 (28-ounce) can tomato sauce

2 cups cooked white rice

1 teaspoon seasoned salt

½ teaspoon black pepper

2 cloves garlic, minced, or 1
teaspoon crushed garlic

## PREPPING FOR THE GRILL

**1.** Cut off the tops of the bell peppers and save for use in the stuffing. Core and remove the seeds from the peppers.

**2.** Finely chop the onion, celery, and bell pepper tops.

**3.** In a 10-inch skillet over medium heat, warm the olive oil and sauté the vegetables for 3 to 4 minutes, until the vegetables are al dente. Remove the vegetables from the pan and set aside.

**4.** Using same skillet, cook the ground beef over medium heat for 8 to 10 minutes, stirring occasionally, until the beef is brown. Drain the fat.

**5.** Set aside ½ cup of tomato sauce to top stuffed peppers.

**6.** Mix the browned ground beef, sautéed vegetables, rice, and remaining tomato sauce in a large bowl. Season with the salt, pepper, and garlic.

**7.** Loosely stuff the bell peppers with the filling and top them with the remaining tomato sauce.

## ON THE WOOD PELLET SMOKER-GRILL

**1.** Configure your wood pellet smoker-grill for indirect cooking and preheat to 180°F using apple or hickory pellets.

**2.** Smoke the bell peppers for 45 minutes.

**3.** After 45 minutes, increase the pit temperature to 350°F, and cook for another 45 minutes.

**4.** Remove the peppers and rest under a foil tent for 10 minutes before serving.

# APPLEWOOD WALNUT-CRUSTED RACK OF LAMB

As you bite through the walnut crust your taste buds will light up when stimulated by a hint of Dijon mustard, garlic, and apple smoke. These juicy lamb chops are smoked to a beautiful medium-rare, giving them a soft and silky texture.

**SERVES: 4**

**PREP TIME:**
25 minutes (plus overnight marinating and 30 minutes rest time)

**COOK TIME:**
60 to 90 minutes

**REST TIME:**
5 minutes

**RECOMMENDED PELLETS: Apple**

3 tablespoons Dijon mustard

2 garlic cloves, minced, or 2 teaspoons crushed garlic

½ teaspoon garlic powder

½ teaspoon kosher salt

½ teaspoon black pepper

½ teaspoon rosemary

1 (1½ to 2-pound) rack of lamb, Frenched

1 cup crushed walnuts

## PREPPING FOR THE GRILL

**1.** Combine the mustard, garlic, garlic powder, salt, pepper, and rosemary in a small bowl.

**2.** Spread the seasoning mix evenly on all sides of the lamb and sprinkle with the crushed walnuts. Press the walnuts lightly with your hand to adhere the nuts to the meat.

**3.** Wrap the walnut-crusted rack of lamb loosely with plastic wrap and refrigerate overnight to allow the seasonings to penetrate the meat.

## ON THE WOOD PELLET SMOKER-GRILL

**1.** Remove the walnut crusted rack of lamb from the refrigerator and rest for 30 minutes to allow it to come to room temperature.

**2.** Configure your wood pellet smoker-grill for indirect cooking and preheat to 225°F using apple pellets.

**3.** Place the rack of lamb bone-side down directly on the grill.

**4.** Smoke at 225°F until the thickest part of the rack of lamb reaches the desired internal temperature, measured with a digital

instant-read thermometer, as you near the times listed in the chart.

**5.** Rest the lamb under a loose foil tent for 5 minutes before serving.

| DONENESS | TEMPERATURE | SMOKE TIME |
|---|---|---|
| Rare | 125°F | about 60 minutes |
| Medium-rare | 130°F | about 70 minutes |
| Medium | 135 to 140°F | about 80 minutes |
| Medium-well | 145°F | about 90 minutes |
| Well-done | 150°F | 90-plus minutes |

**NOTES**

If desired, substitute pistachios for the walnuts.

# ROASTED LEG OF LAMB

Scrumptious roasted leg of lamb will truly delight at any Easter or Passover dinner. But this fuss-free, family-pleasing recipe will have you eating tender and flavorful lamb any time of the year. For best results, do not overcook your lamb.

**SERVES: 8 (½ pound per serving)**

**PREP TIME:**
20 minutes (plus overnight marinating and 1 hour rest times)

**COOK TIME:**
1½ to 2 hours

**REST TIME:**
10 minutes

**RECOMMENDED PELLETS: Any**

1 (4-pound) boneless leg of lamb

½ cup roasted garlic–flavored extra-virgin olive oil

¼ cup dried parsley

3 garlic cloves, minced

2 tablespoons fresh-squeezed lemon juice or 1 tablespoon lemon zest (from 1 medium lemon)

2 tablespoons dried oregano

1 tablespoon dried rosemary

½ teaspoon black pepper

## PREPPING FOR THE GRILL

**1.** Remove any netting from the leg of lamb. Trim any large pieces of gristle, silver skin, and fat.

**2.** In a small bowl, combine the olive oil, parsley, garlic, lemon juice or zest, oregano, rosemary, and pepper.

**3.** Apply the spice rub on the inner and outer surfaces of the boneless leg of lamb.

**4.** Use silicone food-grade cooking bands or butcher's twine to secure the boneless

leg of lamb. Use bands or twine to form and maintain the lamb's basic shape.

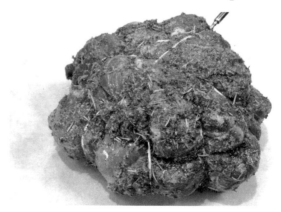

**5.** Wrap the lamb loosely with plastic wrap and refrigerate overnight to allow the seasonings to penetrate the meat.

## ON THE WOOD PELLET SMOKER-GRILL

**1.** Remove the lamb from the refrigerator and let it stand at room temperature for an hour.

**2.** Configure your wood pellet smoker-grill for indirect cooking and preheat to 400°F using your pellets of choice.

**3.** Remove the plastic wrap from the lamb.

**4.** Insert your wood pellet smoker-grill meat probe or a remote meat probe into the thickest part of the lamb. If your grill does not have meat probe capabilities or you don't own a remote meat probe then use an instant-read digital thermometer during the cook for internal temperature readings. Roast the lamb at 400°F until the internal temperature at the thickest part reaches desired doneness.

**5.** Rest the lamb under a loose foil tent for 10 minutes before carving against the grain and serving.

| DONENESS | TEMPERATURE | VISUAL CUES |
|----------|-------------|-------------|
| Rare | 120° to 125°F | Center is bright red, pink toward the center |
| Medium-rare | 130° to 135°F | Center is very pink, slightly brown toward the center |
| Medium | 140° to 145°F | Center is light pink, outer edges are brown |
| Medium-well | 150° to 155°F | Not pink |
| Well-done | 160°F and above | Uniformly brown throughout |

**NOTES**

Do not bring the roast directly from the refrigerator to your wood pellet smoker-grill; the roast must be at room temperature to ensure it will cook evenly.

When roasted to medium-rare, lamb is flavorful and mild like a roast beef.

Pesto sauce can be substituted for the spice rub.

# CHAPTER 4
# PORK

# SMOKED PORK TENDERLOINS

Seasoned pitmasters and novices alike can agree that this cut of pork is the most tender portion. Pork tenderloins cooked correctly are very moist and delectable. They are so tender you can literally cut them with a fork! Tenderloins are relatively lean, and need not be cooked over 145°F.

Smoke the tenderloin before finishing at 350°F for that extra-delicious savory touch.

**SERVES: 4 to 6 per pork tenderloin**

| **PREP TIME:** | **COOK TIME:** | **REST TIME:** |
| --- | --- | --- |
| **20 minutes (plus 2 to 4 hours marinating)** | **1½ hours** | **10 minutes** |

**RECOMMENDED PELLETS: Hickory, Apple**

2 (1½ to 2-pound) pork tenderloins

¼ cup roasted garlic-flavored extra-virgin olive oil

¼ cup Jan's Original Dry Rub (page 168) or Pork Dry Rub (page 169)

## PREPPING FOR THE GRILL

**1.** Trim any excess fat and silver skin from the meat.

**2.** Rub all sides of the tenderloins with the olive oil and dust with the rub.

**3.** Wrap the seasoned tenderloins in plastic wrap and refrigerate for 2 to 4 hours.

## ON THE WOOD PELLET SMOKER-GRILL

**1.** Configure your wood pellet smoker-grill for indirect cooking and preheat to 230°F using hickory or apple pellets.

**2.** Remove the plastic wrap from the meat and insert your wood pellet smoker-grill probes or a remote meat probe into the thickest part of each tenderloin. If your grill does not have meat probe capabilities or you don't own a remote meat probe then use an instant-read digital thermometer during the cook for internal temperature readings.

**3.** Place the tenderloins directly on the grill and smoke them for 45 minutes at 230°F.

**4.** Increase the pit temperature to 350°F and finish cooking the tenderloins for about 45 more minutes, until the internal temperature at the thickest part reaches 145°F.

**5.** Rest the pork tenderloins under a loose foil tent for 10 minutes before serving.

**NOTES**

Pork tenderloins normally come two per package, giving you the option of cooking both or vacuum-sealing and freezing the second one for later use.

It's best to remove the silver skin because it is very tough and prevents rub from penetrating the tenderloin.

# PULLED HICKORY-SMOKED PORK BUTTS

Pulled hickory-smoked pork butts produce moist shreds of succulent pork mixed with strongly seasoned bark (the jerkylike, crusty, chewy, dark, rich, outer shell of the butt). It's perfect for feeding large groups, and the leftovers freeze and reheat extremely well for tacos, enchiladas, burritos, nachos, pizzas, casseroles...the list is endless!

This recipe uses a technique I call the "Turbo method" which involves wrapping pork butts in foil during the cook in order to bypass the dreaded stall (page 24) while still providing a great bark. It also cooks the pork butts in approximately 6 hours rather than 12 to 16 hours.

**SERVES: 20 or more**

| **PREP TIME:** | **COOK TIME:** | **REST TIME:** |
|---|---|---|
| 30 to 45 minutes (plus overnight marinating) | 6 hours | 3 to 4 hours |

**RECOMMENDED PELLETS: Hickory**

2 (10-pound) boneless pork butts, vacuum-packed or fresh

1 cup roasted garlic–flavored extra-virgin olive oil

¾ cup Pork Dry Rub (page 169), Jan's Original Dry Rub (page 168), or your favorite pork rub

## PREPPING FOR THE GRILL

**1.** Trim the fat cap and any easily accessible large portions of excess fat from each pork butt as you see fit. Some pitmasters prefer to trim the fat cap to ¼ inch or leave the entire fat cap on because they believe that the melting fat bastes the butts as they cook. This method inhibits the formation of bark in areas covered by fat. Therefore I recommend removing the fat cap to maximize the amount of cherished bark.

**2.** Cut each pork butt in half. Use silicone food-grade cooking bands or butcher's twine to hold the meat together during cooking and handling.

**3.** Rub all the sides of each pork butt with the oil. Sprinkle each pork butt with a liberal amount of the rub and pat it in with your hand.

**4.** Individually double-wrap the seasoned boneless pork butts tightly in plastic wrap and refrigerate overnight.

## ON THE WOOD PELLET SMOKER-GRILL

**1.** Configure your wood pellet smoker-grill for indirect cooking and preheat to 225°F using hickory pellets.

**2.** Remove the pork butts from the refrigerator and remove the plastic wrap while preheating your wood pellet smoker-grill. The pork butts don't need to fully come to room temperature. Insert your wood pellet smoker-grill meat probes or a remote meat probe into the thickest part of one or more pork butts. If your grill does not have meat probe capabilities or you don't own a remote meat probe, then use an instant-read digital thermometer during the cook for internal temperature readings.

**3.** Smoke the pork butts for 3 hours.

**4.** After 3 hours, increase the pit temperature to 350°F and cook until the internal temperature of the butts reaches 160°F.

**5.** Remove the pork butts from the grill and double-wrap each one in heavy-duty aluminum foil. Take care to make sure that you keep your meat probes in the butts as you double-wrap them.

**6.** Return the wrapped pork butts to your 350°F pellet smoker grill.

**7.** Continue cooking the foil-wrapped pork butts until the internal temperature of the pork butts reaches 200° to 205°F.

**8.** Remove the pork butts and FTC (page 20) them for 3 to 4 hours before pulling and serving.

**9.** Pull the smoked pork butts into little succulent shreds using your favorite pulling method. I prefer using my hands while wearing heat-resistant gloves.

**10.** If you'd like, mix the pulled pork butts with any remaining liquids.

**11.** Serve the pulled pork with barbecue sauce on a fresh-baked roll topped with coleslaw, or serve the pulled pork with condiments like lettuce, tomato, red onion, mayo, cheese, and horseradish.

**NOTES**

I prefer to slather my pork butts with extra-virgin olive oil to act as the glue for the rub, but you can substitute yellow mustard, molasses, Carolina Treet Cooking Barbecue Sauce, or even Worcestershire sauce for equally wonderful results.

Every large chunk of meat like a pork butt (shoulder) or beef brisket smoked and roasted low and slow will go through "the stall" (page 24). This recipe however, uses the Texas crutch technique (page 25) to overcome that.

# PORK SIRLOIN TIP ROAST THREE WAYS

I've found the most incredibly tender and juicy pork sirloin tip roasts at Costco. These roasts lend themselves well to various cooking methods and accept a multitude of rubs, seasonings, marinades, and injections. Sirloin tip roasts are cut from the leg area and are said to be the equivalent of a beef tri-tip roast. Ask your local butcher to locate them for you. I guarantee you'll love these versatile little roasts.

**SERVES: 4 to 6**

| **PREP TIME:** | **COOK TIME:** | **REST TIME:** |
|---|---|---|
| 20 minutes (plus overnight marinating) | 1½ to 3 hours, depending on method | 15 minutes |

**RECOMMENDED PELLETS: Apple, Hickory**

## APPLE-INJECTED ROASTED PORK SIRLOIN TIP ROAST

1 (1½ to 2-pound) pork sirloin tip roast

¾ cup 100% apple juice

2 tablespoons roasted garlic-flavored extra-virgin olive oil

5 tablespoons Pork Dry Rub (page 169) or a commercial rub such as Plowboys BBQ Bovine Bold

## PREPPING FOR THE GRILL

**1.** Pat the roast dry with a paper towel.

**2.** Use a flavor/marinade injector to inject all areas of tip roast with the apple juice.

**3.** Rub the entire roast with the olive oil and then coat liberally with the rub.

**4.** Use 2 silicone food-grade cooking bands or butcher's twine to truss the roast.

**5.** Wrap the tip roast in plastic wrap and refrigerate overnight.

## ON THE WOOD PELLET SMOKER-GRILL

**1.** Remove the roast from the refrigerator and rest it on the counter while preheating your pit.

**2.** Configure your wood pellet smoker-grill for indirect cooking and preheat to 350°F using apple pellets.

**3.** Remove the plastic wrap and insert your wood pellet smoker-grill meat probe or a remote meat probe into the thickest part of the roast. If your grill does not have meat probe capabilities or you don't own a remote meat probe, then use an instant-read digital thermometer during the cook for internal temperature readings.

**4.** Roast the meat until the internal temperature reaches 145°F, about 1½ hours.

**5.** Rest the roast under a loose foil tent for 15 minutes.

**6.** Remove the cooking bands or twine, and carve the roast against the grain.

# TERIYAKI-MARINATED PORK SIRLOIN TIP ROAST

1 (1½ to 2-pound) pork sirloin tip roast

Teriyaki marinade such as Mr. Yoshida's Original Gourmet Marinade

## PREPPING FOR THE GRILL

**1.** Pat the roast dry with a paper towel.

**2.** Using a 1-gallon freezer storage bag or a sealable container, cover the roast with the teriyaki marinade.

**3.** Refrigerate overnight, rotating every few hours when possible.

## ON THE WOOD PELLET SMOKER-GRILL

**1.** Remove the roast from the refrigerator and the marinade, and pat it dry. Truss the roast using 2 to 3 silicone food-grade cooking bands or butcher's twine to make sure the roast maintains its shape during cooking.

**2.** Rest the marinated sirloin tip roast on the counter while preheating your wood pellet smoker-grill.

**3.** Insert your wood pellet smoker-grill meat probe or a remote meat probe into the thickest part of the roast. If your grill does not have meat probe capabilities or you don't own a remote meat probe, then use an instant-read digital thermometer during the cook for internal temperature readings.

**4.** Configure your wood pellet smoker-grill for indirect cooking and preheat to 180°F using hickory pellets.

**5.** Smoke the meat roast for 1 hour at 180°F.

**6.** After an hour, increase your pit temperature to 325°F.

**7.** Cook the roast until the internal temperature, at the thickest part of the roast, reaches 145°F, about 1 to 1½ hours.

**8.** Rest the roast under a loose foil tent for 15 minutes.

**9.** Remove the cooking bands or twine, and carve the roast against the grain.

## HICKORY-SMOKED PORK SIRLOIN TIP ROAST

1 (1½ to 2-pound) pork sirloin tip roast

2 tablespoons roasted garlic–flavored extra-virgin olive oil

5 tablespoons Jan's Original Dry Rub (page 168), Pork Dry Rub (page 169), or your favorite pork rub

### PREPPING FOR THE GRILL

**1.** Pat the roast dry with a paper towel.

**2.** Rub the entire roast with the olive oil. Coat the roast with the rub.

**3.** Truss the roast using 2 to 3 silicone food-grade cooking bands or butcher's twine to make sure the roast maintains its shape during cooking.

**4.** Wrap the tip roast in plastic wrap and refrigerate overnight.

## ON THE WOOD PELLET SMOKER-GRILL

**1.** Remove the sirloin tip roast from the refrigerator and rest the roast on the counter while preheating the grill.

**2.** Configure your wood pellet smoker-grill for indirect cooking and preheat to 225°F with hickory pellets.

**3.** Remove the plastic wrap and insert your wood pellet smoker-grill meat probe or a remote meat probe into the thickest part of the roast. If your grill does not have meat probe capabilities or you don't own a remote meat probe, then use an instant-read digital thermometer during the cook for internal temperature readings.

**4.** Place the roast directly on the grill grates and smoke the roast until the internal temperature, at the thickest part of the roast, reaches 145°F, about 3 hours.

**5.** Rest the roast under a loose foil tent for 15 minutes.

**6.** Remove the cooking bands or twine, and carve the roast against the grain.

# DOUBLE-SMOKED HAM

Double-smoking an applewood-smoked, boneless, fully cooked, ready-to-eat ham adds a new dimension to any Easter, Christmas, or Sunday dinner. You'll notice a remarkable difference from merely cooking the ham in your oven. Double-smoking works equally well with bone-in hickory-smoked hams. This recipe uses a fully cooked, ready-to-eat ham and enhances the flavor by re-smoking the ham before heating it to temperature.

**SERVES: 8 to 12**

**PREP TIME:**
15 minutes (plus 30 minutes rest time)

**COOK TIME:**
2½ to 3 hours

**REST TIME:**
15 minutes

**RECOMMENDED PELLETS: Apple, Hickory**

1 (10-pound) applewood-smoked, boneless, fully cooked, ready-to-eat ham or bone-in smoked ham

## PREPPING FOR THE GRILL

**1.** Remove the ham from its packaging and let sit at room temperature for 30 minutes.

## ON THE WOOD PELLET SMOKER-GRILL

**1.** Configure your wood pellet smoker-grill for indirect cooking and preheat to 180°F using apple or hickory pellets depending on what type of wood was used for the initial smoking.

**2.** Place the ham directly on the grill grates and smoke the ham for 1 hour at 180°F.

**3.** After an hour, increase pit temperature to 350°F.

**4.** Cook the ham until the internal temperature reaches 140°F, about 1½ to 2 more hours.

**5.** Remove the ham and wrap in foil for 15 minutes before carving against the grain.

**NOTES**

Pay close attention to the difference between "Ready to Eat" and "Ready to Cook" hams. The main difference is that the "Ready to Eat" hams are fully cooked and only need to be taken to an internal temperature of 140°F, but "Ready to Cook" hams are only partially cooked and need to be taken to an internal temperature of 160°F.

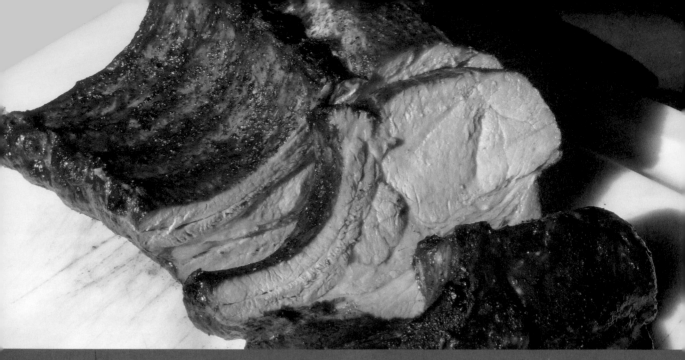

# HICKORY-SMOKED PRIME RIB OF PORK

Impress your family and guests with a prime rib of pork seasoned to perfection and slow-smoked with hickory. This roast will deliver the most tender, flavorful cut of pork you'll ever have. Its counterpart is a standing beef rib roast or a rack of lamb.

**SERVES: 6**

**PREP TIME:**
**30 minutes (plus 2 to 4 hours or overnight marinating)**

**COOK TIME:**
**3 to 3½ hours**

**REST TIME:**
**15 minutes**

**RECOMMENDED PELLETS: Hickory**

1 (5-pound) rack of pork, about 6 ribs

¼ cup roasted garlic–flavored extra-virgin olive oil

6 tablespoons Jan's Original Dry Rub (page 168), Pork Dry Rub (page 169), or your favorite pork roast rub

## PREPPING FOR THE GRILL

**1.** Trim off the fat cap and silver skin from the rack of pork. Just like a slab of ribs, a rack of pork has a membrane on the bones. Remove the membrane from the bones by working a spoon handle under the bone membrane until you can grab the membrane with a paper towel to pull it off.

**2.** Rub the olive oil liberally on all sides of the meat. Season with the rub, covering all sides of the meat.

**3.** Double wrap the seasoned rack of pork in plastic wrap and refrigerate for 2 to 4 hours or overnight.

## ON THE WOOD PELLET SMOKER-GRILL

**1.** Remove the seasoned rack of pork from the refrigerator and let sit at room temperature for 30 minutes before cooking.

**2.** Configure your wood pellet smoker-grill for indirect cooking and preheat to 225°F using hickory pellets.

**3.** Insert your wood pellet smoker-grill meat probe or a remote meat probe into the thickest part of the rack of pork. If your grill does not have meat probe capabilities or you don't own a remote meat

probe then, use an instant-read digital thermometer during the cook for internal temperature readings.

**4.** Place the rack rib-side down directly on the grill grates.

**5.** Smoke the rack of pork for 3 to 3½ hours, until the internal temperature reaches 140°F.

**6.** Remove from the meat from the smoker, and let it rest under a loose foil tent for 15 minutes before carving.

**NOTES**

The prime rib of pork is composed of the pork sirloin and baby back ribs. The prime rib of pork is also known as a rack of pork or pork rib roast.

# TENDER GRILLED LOIN CHOPS

The secret to tender, extra-meaty pork loin chops is to ensure they are at least 1-inch thick. The best way is to cut them yourself from a whole pork loin (see note on page 129). Brushing your loin chops with extra-virgin olive oil seals in the natural juices as the chops grill. Be careful not to overcook the chops.

**SERVES: 6**

| **PREP TIME:** | **COOK TIME:** | **REST TIME:** |
| --- | --- | --- |
| **10 minutes (plus optional 12 to 24 hours brining)** | **12 to 15 minutes** | **5 minutes** |

**RECOMMENDED PELLETS: Any**

6 boneless center-cut loin pork chops, 1 to 1½ inches thick

2 quarts Pork Brine (page 165)

2 tablespoons roasted garlic-flavored extra-virgin olive oil

2 teaspoons black pepper

## PREPPING FOR THE GRILL

**1.** Trim excess fat and silver skin from the pork chops.

**2.** Place the pork chops and brine in a 1-gallon sealable bag and refrigerate for at least 12 hours or overnight.

**3.** Remove the pork chops from the brine, and pat them dry with paper towels.

**4.** Rub each pork chop with the olive oil on all sides, and season all sides with the pepper. Do not salt the brined pork chops before grilling, as the brine provides the necessary salt.

**5.** Allow the pork chops to rest while the wood pellet smoker-grill is preheating.

## ON THE WOOD PELLET SMOKER-GRILL

**1.** Use searing grates to configure your wood pellet smoker-grill for direct cooking. Spray the surface of the grates with cooking spray.

**2.** Set the grill to high and preheat to at least 450°F using any pellets.

**3.** Sear the pork chops for 3 minutes on one side.

**4.** Rotate the pork chops 90 degrees to achieve those aesthetically pleasing cross grill marks.

**5.** Grill the chops for an additional 3 minutes.

**6.** Flip the pork chops and continue grilling until the internal temperature reaches 145°F, 6 to 8 more minutes.

**7.** Brined pork chops cook faster than un-brined chops, so be careful to monitor internal temperatures.

**8.** Rest the pork chops under a foil tent for 5 minutes before serving.

**NOTES**

I recommend using a pig tail food flipper to rotate and flip meat rather than tongs. With tongs, you might apply too much pressure while squeezing the pork chops, causing succulent juices to escape.

# FLORENTINE RIBEYE PORK LOIN

This delicious and impressive Florentine ribeye pork loin is extremely simple to put together, and you'll enjoy the flavorful stuffing of spinach, mozzarella, bacon, and onion.

**SERVES: 6 to 8**

**PREP TIME:**
30 minutes

**COOK TIME:**
60 to 75 minutes

**REST TIME:**
15 minutes

**RECOMMENDED PELLETS: Any**

1 (3-pound) boneless
ribeye pork loin roast

4 tablespoons extra-virgin
olive oil, divided

2 tablespoons Pork Dry Rub (page
169) or your favorite pork seasoning

4 bacon slices

6 cups fresh spinach

1 small red onion, diced

6 cloves garlic, cut into thin slivers

¾ cup shredded mozzarella cheese

## PREPPING FOR THE GRILL

**1.** Trim away any excess fat and silver skin.

**2.** Butterfly the pork loin or ask your butcher to butterfly it for you. There are many excellent videos online with detailed instructions on the different techniques for butterflying a loin roast.

**3.** Rub 2 tablespoons of the olive oil on each side of the butterflied roast, and season both sides with the rub.

**4.** Cook the bacon in a large skillet over medium heat. Crumble and set aside. Reserve the bacon fat.

**5.** In a large skillet over medium-high heat, heat 2 tablespoons of the reserved bacon fat, wilt the spinach, and set aside.

**6.** Using the same large skillet over medium-high heat, heat 2 additional tablespoons of bacon fat and cook the onion until it is translucent, about 8 minutes.

**7.** Layer the wilted spinach, garlic slivers, shredded mozzarella, crumbled bacon, and onion in the center of the butterflied pork loin.

**8.** Roll the butterflied pork loin tightly. Tie off the stuffed ribeye pork loin with butcher's twine at 2-inch intervals.

## ON THE WOOD PELLET SMOKER-GRILL

**1.** Configure your wood pellet smoker-grill for indirect cooking and preheat to 375°F using any pellets.

**2.** Insert your wood pellet smoker-grill meat probe or a remote meat probe into the thickest part of the pork loin. If your grill does not have meat probe capabilities or you don't own a remote meat probe, then use an instant-read digital thermometer during the cook for internal temperature readings.

**3.** Grill the pork loin for 60 to 75 minutes, or until the internal temperature at the thickest part reaches 140°F.

**4.** Rest the pork loin under a loose foil tent for 15 minutes before carving against the grain.

**NOTES**

The ribeye portion of a pork loin is characterized by the marbled fat.

You can substitute the sirloin portion of a pork loin for this recipe.

There are many excellent video online showing how to butterfly a pork loin. Here is one I find very approachable: http://bit.ly/S4YM5B.

# NAKED ST. LOUIS RIBS

Naked St. Louis–style ribs are smoked low and slow without barbecue sauce, allowing the true flavor profiles of the rub and meaty pork ribs to shine. St. Louis ribs are trimmed-down spare ribs and are bigger and a bit tougher than baby back ribs. However, you'll love the results once the fat has been rendered out.

**SERVES: 6 to 8**

**PREP TIME:**
**30 minutes**

**COOK TIME:**
**5 to 6 hours**

**REST TIME:**
**10 minutes**

**RECOMMENDED PELLETS: Hickory, Apple**

3 St. Louis-style pork rib racks

1 cup plus 1 tablespoon Jan's
Original Dry Rub (page 168)
or your favorite pork rub

## PREPPING FOR THE GRILL

**1.** Remove the membrane on the underside of the rib racks by inserting a spoon handle between the membrane and rib bones. Grab the membrane with a paper towel and slowly pull it down the rack to remove.

**2.** Rub both sides of the ribs with a liberal amount of the rub.

## ON THE WOOD PELLET SMOKER-GRILL

**1.** Configure your wood pellet smoker-grill for indirect cooking and preheat to 225°F using hickory or apple pellets.

**2.** If using a rib rack, place the ribs in the rack on the grill grates. Otherwise you can use Teflon-coated fiberglass mats, or place the ribs directly on the grill grates.

**3.** Smoke the ribs at 225°F for 5 to 6 hours with hickory pellets until the internal temperature, at the thickest part of the ribs, reaches 185°F to 190°F.

**4.** Rest the ribs under a loose foil tent for 10 minutes before carving and serving.

**NOTES**

Perform the following rib tests to check for doneness:

- The internal temperature should be 185° to 190°F.
- Pick up the rack in the center with tongs—the rack should bend into a U-shape.
- The meat should pull off the bone and not fall off the bone.

# BUTTERMILK PORK SIRLOIN ROAST

A sirloin roast is cut from the back of the loin area and lends itself well to low-and-slow cooking. With low calories and fat, the sirloin is considered very lean, so care must be taken to avoid drying it out. The tender and moist results will have friends and family begging you to make it again.

**SERVES: 4 to 6**

**PREP TIME:**
20 minutes (plus marinating overnight)

**COOK TIME:**
3 to 3½ hours

**REST TIME:**
15 minutes

**RECOMMENDED PELLETS: Apple, Cherry**

1 (3 to 3½-pound) pork sirloin roast

1 quart Buttermilk Brine (page 166)

## PREPPING FOR THE GRILL

**1.** Trim all fat and silver skin from the pork roast.

**2.** Place the roast and buttermilk brine in a 1-gallon sealable plastic bag or brining container.

**3.** Refrigerate overnight, rotating the roast every few hours when possible.

## ON THE WOOD PELLET SMOKER-GRILL

**1.** Remove the brined pork sirloin roast from the brine and pat dry with a paper towel.

**2.** Insert a meat probe into the thickest part of the roast.

**3.** Configure your wood pellet smoker-grill for indirect cooking and preheat to 225°F using apple or cherry pellets.

**4.** Smoke the roast until the internal temperature reaches 145°F, 3 to 3½ hours.

**5.** Rest the roast under a loose foil tent for 15 minutes, then carve against the grain.

**NOTES**

Butchering a whole boneless pork loin is extremely economical and affords you many options. The cut on the bottom left is considered the sirloin portion, while the cut on the bottom right is the ribeye (note the marbled fat). The center cut is considered the steak. Cut the steak portion into 2-inch thick chops. Each portion will easily feed three to four people. You'll be amazed at the savings you'll achieve.

# CHAPTER 5
# SEAFOOD

# BAKED FRESH WILD SOCKEYE SALMON

Sockeye salmon (known as "reds" because of their dark red-orange meat) has a bold, rich flavor and a juicy, firm texture. This recipe pulls together easily and produces very tender, flaky salmon in about 30 minutes. Since sockeye salmon has such firm flesh, it stands up really well to baking and grilling.

**SERVES: 6**

**PREP TIME:**
**15 minutes**

**COOK TIME:**
**15 to 20 minutes**

**REST TIME:**
**5 minutes**

**RECOMMENDED PELLETS: Any**

2 fresh wild sockeye salmon
fillets, skin on

2 teaspoons Seafood
Seasoning (page 170)

¾ teaspoon Old Bay seasoning

## PREPPING FOR THE GRILL

**1.** Rinse the salmon fillets with cold water and pat them dry with a paper towel.

**2.** Lightly dust the fillets with the seasonings.

## ON THE WOOD PELLET SMOKER-GRILL

**1.** Configure your wood pellet smoker-grill for indirect cooking and preheat to 400°F using any pellets.

**2.** Lay the salmon skin-side down on a Teflon-coated fiberglass mat or directly on the grill grates.

**3.** Bake the salmon for 15 to 20 minutes, until the internal temperature reaches 140°F and/or the flesh flakes easily with a fork.

**4.** Rest the salmon for 5 minutes before serving.

### NOTES

This recipe works equally well with Chinook (king), coho (silver), pink (humpback), or farmed Atlantic salmon.

Salmon tends to dry easily when baking, so bake it skin-side down to help retain moisture.

# ALDER CREOLE WILD PACIFIC ROCKFISH

Transport yourself to the Louisiana bayous with this Creole rockfish recipe. Over 70 varieties of basslike fish from North America's West Coast can be referred to as Pacific rockfish. Rockfish are firm, lean, and mild-flavored, and lend themselves well to baking and frying. But as I discovered, they can be smoked as well, with excellent results.

**SERVES: 4**

| PREP TIME: | COOK TIME: | REST TIME: |
|---|---|---|
| 15 minutes | 90 minutes | 5 minutes |

**RECOMMENDED PELLETS:** Alder

4 to 7 (4 to 6-ounce) fresh, wild Pacific rockfish fillets

3 teaspoons roasted garlic–flavored extra-virgin olive oil

2 tablespoons Creole Seafood Seasoning (page 167) or any Creole seasoning

## PREPPING FOR THE GRILL

**1.** Rub both sides of the fillets with the olive oil.

**2.** Dust both sides with the seasoning.

## ON THE WOOD PELLET SMOKER-GRILL

**1.** Configure your wood pellet smoker-grill for indirect cooking and preheat to 225°F using alder pellets.

**2.** Place the fillets on a Teflon-coated fiberglass mat to prevent them from sticking to the grill grates.

**3.** Smoke the fillets for approximately 90 minutes, until they reach an internal temperature of 140°F and/or the flesh flakes easily with a fork.

**4.** Let the fillets rest for 5 minutes before serving.

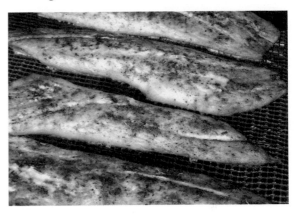

**NOTES**

You can also bake the fillets in your wood pellet smoker-grill on a Teflon-coated fiberglass mat at 350°F for 25 to 40 minutes, until the internal temperature reaches 140°F and/or the flesh flakes easily with a fork.

# SHRIMP-STUFFED TILAPIA

This easy-to-prepare seafood lover's delight brings restaurant-quality elegance to any dinner table.

**SERVES: 5**

**PREP TIME:**
**20 minutes**

**COOK TIME:**
**30 to 45 minutes**

**REST TIME:**
**5 minutes**

**RECOMMENDED PELLETS: Any**

5 (4 to 6-ounce) fresh, farmed tilapia fillets

2 tablespoons extra-virgin olive oil

**FOR THE SHRIMP STUFFING:**

1 pound cooked, peeled, deveined, tail-off shrimp

1 tablespoon salted butter

1 cup finely diced red onion

1 cup Italian bread crumbs

½ cup mayonnaise

1½ teaspoons smoked paprika

1½ teaspoons Seafood Seasoning (page 170) or Old Bay seasoning

1 large egg, beaten

2 teaspoons fresh chopped parsley or dried parsley

1½ teaspoons Fagundes Famous Seasoning or salt and pepper

## PREPPING FOR THE GRILL

**1.** Prepare the shrimp stuffing. Use a food processor, salsa maker, or knife to finely chop the shrimp.

**2.** In a small skillet over medium-high heat, melt the butter and sauté the red onion until translucent, about 3 minutes. Set aside and let cool to room temperature.

**3.** Combine the shrimp, cooled sautéed onion, and remaining ingredients in a large bowl.

**4.** Cover and refrigerate the shrimp stuffing until ready to use. Use shrimp stuffing within 2 days.

**5.** Rub both sides of the fillets with the olive oil.

**6.** Spoon ⅓ cup of the stuffing onto the back side of each fillet. The back side of the tilapia fillet has reddish stripping.

**7.** Flatten out the stuffing on the bottom half of the fillet. Fold the tilapia in half and secure with 2 or more toothpicks to hold the fish in place.

**8.** Dust each fillet with the smoked paprika and seafood seasoning or Old Bay seasoning.

## ON THE WOOD PELLET SMOKER-GRILL

**1.** Configure your wood pellet smoker-grill for indirect cooking and preheat to 400°F using any pellets.

**2.** Place the stuffed fillets on a nonstick grilling tray.

**3.** Bake the tilapia for 30 to 45 minutes, or until they reach an internal temperature of 145°F and the fish flakes easily.

**4.** Rest the fish for 5 minutes before serving.

**NOTES**

Cooking time depends on the thickness of the fillets.

Nonstick grilling trays are great for vegetables and fish.

Store extra shrimp stuffing in refrigerator for later use with other recipes or as a wonderful shrimp-cake hors d'oeuvre. Using ⅓ cup of stuffing, form thin patties and pan fry them for a few minutes in extra-virgin olive oil or vegetable oil. They make nice tidbits for the pitmaster and friends!

# COLD-HOT SMOKED SALMON

This brined authentic Northwest alder wood–smoked salmon recipe uses both cold and hot smoking processes in order to slowly and fully cook the salmon to an internal temperature of 145°F. True cold-smoked salmon is cured and actually is still raw.

**SERVES: 4**

**PREP TIME:**
16 hours (8 hours brining and 8 hours drying)

**COOK TIME:**
8 hours

**REST TIME:**
10 minutes

**RECOMMENDED PELLETS: Alder**

5 pounds fresh sockeye (red), Chinook (King), coho (silver), or Atlantic farmed salmon fillets

4 cups Salmon and Trout Brine (page 166)

## PREPPING FOR THE GRILL

**1.** Cut salmon fillets into 3 to 4-inch square pieces so that they will smoke/cook at the same rate.

**2.** Place the salmon pieces into a 1-gallon food-grade plastic bag or brining container and refrigerate for 8 hours. Rotate the salmon every 2 hours to make sure it remains submerged.

**3.** Remove the salmon from the brine and lightly pat the pieces dry with a paper towel.

**4.** Air-dry the brined salmon in the refrigerator, uncovered, for 8 hours to allow the pellicle (see notes) to form.

## ON THE WOOD PELLET SMOKER-GRILL

**1.** Configure your wood pellet smoker-grill for indirect cooking. If your grill has cold-smoking capabilities, then configure your pellet smoker-grill for cold-smoking.

**2.** Remove the salmon pieces from refrigerator and place them on Teflon-coated fiberglass mats.

**3.** Preheat your wood pellet smoker-grill to 180°F using alder pellets. A pit temperature of 180°F should result in a cold-smoke temperature of 70° to 100°F in your smoker box, depending on the ambient temperature.

**4.** Smoke the salmon using the following pit temperatures, which should result in the listed smoke box temperatures:

- Pellet smoker-grill set point at 180°F: Smoke salmon for 1 hour—box temp 80°F to 90°F.

- Pellet smoker-grill set point at 225°F: Smoke salmon for 1 hour—box temp 110°F.

- Pellet smoker-grill set point at 250°F: Smoke salmon for 2 hours—box temp 120°F.

- Pellet smoker-grill set point at 350°F: Smoke salmon for 2 to 4 hours—box temp 150°F to 160°F.

- The smoker box temperature needs to stay below 175°F.

**5.** Continue smoking the salmon until the internal temperature of the salmon at the thickest part reaches 145°F.

**6.** Remove the salmon from the grill and let rest for 10 minutes before serving.

**7.** Vacuum-seal any remaining smoked salmon and freeze for up to 6 months. Vacuum-sealing and freezing smoked salmon actually enhances the alder-smoked flavor.

**NOTES**

Salmon fillets should be free of bones, but always take care when eating fish.

The pellicle, or the formation of a tacky skin, plays an important role in producing excellent smoked fish by acting as a protective barrier yet allowing the fish to capture the color and smoky flavor of alder.

A long-time favorite for smoking fish in the Pacific Northwest, alder wood adds a mild yet distinct flavor, with a hint of sweetness.

Keep the smoker box vent fully open to allow moisture to escape.

# HOT-SMOKED TERIYAKI TUNA

I developed this hot-smoked recipe to achieve similar results as cold-smoking. Cold-smoking occurs at temperatures below 100°F. Unless your wood pellet smoker-grill has a separate smoking chamber like the MAK Grills 2 Star Super Smoker Box, it will be challenging to do any cold smoking. Many wood pellet smoker-grills do not have the ability to operate below 170°F. This recipe can be used with most fish like salmon, tuna, halibut, and Pacific rockfish.

**SERVES: 4**

| PREP TIME: | COOK TIME: | REST TIME: |
|---|---|---|
| **5 to 7 hours (3 hours brining and 2 to 4 hours drying)** | **2 hours** | **10 minutes** |

**RECOMMENDED PELLETS: Alder**

2 (10-ounce) fresh tuna steaks

2 cups Mr. Yoshida's Traditional Teriyaki Marinade and Cooking Sauce, or any other teriyaki marinade

## PREPPING FOR THE GRILL

**1.** Slice the tuna into uniformly thick slices, approximately 2 inches thick.

**2.** Place the tuna slices in a 1-gallon sealable plastic bag along with the marinade and place it in a shallow baking dish in case of a leak. Let sit in the refrigerator for 3 hours, rotating the tuna every hour.

**3.** After 3 hours, remove the tuna from the marinade and lightly pat it dry with a paper towel.

**4.** Allow the tuna to air-dry, uncovered, in the refrigerator for 2 to 4 hours until pellicles form (see note on page 141 for more information).

## ON THE WOOD PELLET SMOKER-GRILL

**1.** Configure your wood pellet smoker-grill for indirect cooking and preheat to 180°F using alder pellets.

**2.** Place the tuna pieces on a Teflon-coated fiberglass mat or directly on the grill grates, and smoke the tuna for an hour.

**3.** After 1 hour, increase the pit temperature to 250°F. Cook for about 1 hour more, until the internal temperature reaches 145°F.

**4.** Remove the tuna from the grill and let rest for 10 minutes before serving.

**NOTES**
Ensure that the tuna slices are the same size so that they will smoke at the same rate.

# SMOKED SALMON & DUNGENESS CRAB CHOWDER

While camping, crabbing, and fishing at Winchester Bay on the Oregon Coast, I came up with this quick and easy chowder recipe that uses Dungeness crabmeat and freshly smoked salmon. The sweet and tender Dungeness crab is a wonderful complement to smoked salmon. This stunning alternative to clam chowder makes an excellent starter to any meal.

**SERVES: 6 (as an appetizer)**

| PREP TIME: | COOK TIME: | REST TIME: |
|---|---|---|
| 30 minutes | 40 minutes | 5 minutes |

4 gallons plus 5 cups water

3 fresh Dungeness crabs

1 cup rock salt

3 cups fresh or leftover frozen, thawed Cold-Hot Smoked Salmon (page 139), divided

3 cups ocean clam juice

5 celery stalks, diced

1 small yellow onion, diced

2 large russet potatoes, peeled and diced

1 (14-ounce) can sweet corn, drained

1 (12-ounce) package clam chowder dry soup mix or creamy potato dry soup mix

4 bacon slices, cooked and crumbled

## PREPPING FOR THE GRILL

**1.** Bring the 4 gallons of water and the rock salt to a rapid boil. Place the fresh Dungeness crabs in the boiling water. Once water returns to a boil, cover and boil the crabs for 20 minutes. Remove the crabs from water and set aside to cool. Once cooled, clean the crabs thoroughly and pick the crabmeat from the shells.

**2.** Flake the freshly smoked salmon.

**3.** In a large uncovered pot over high heat, bring the clam juice, remaining 5 cups water, diced celery, diced potatoes, and onion to a hard boil. Once it reaches a boil, turn down the heat to a medium simmer, and let cook for 10 minutes.

**4.** Add the corn, return the liquid to a boil, and whisk in the clam chowder or creamy potato mix until all the lumps are gone.

**5.** Simmer on low for 15 minutes, stirring the chowder often.

**6.** In the last 5 minutes, add the crumbled bacon.

**7.** Garnish each serving of chowder with ½ cup of flaked smoked salmon and ½ cup of Dungeness crabmeat.

**NOTES**

Store fresh crabmeat no longer than 5 days in the refrigerator.

# ALDER WOOD–SMOKED BONED TROUT

Alder wood–smoked boned trout has an awesome, delicate flavor that can be served as a main dish, an appetizer, substituted for clams in your favorite chowder recipe, crumbled in salads, or added to cream cheese for dips. Trout's silky texture lends itself perfectly to being cold or hot-smoked. You'll love the flavor produced by the brining process and alder wood smoke.

**SERVES: 4**

**PREP TIME:**
**4 hours (2 hours brining and 2 hours drying)**

**COOK TIME:**
**2½ hours**

**REST TIME:**
**5 minutes**

**RECOMMENDED PELLETS: Alder**

4 fresh boned whole trout, skin on and pin bones removed

5 cups Salmon and Trout Brine (page 166)

## PREPPING FOR THE GRILL

**1.** Place the trout in a 2-gallon sealable plastic bag or brining container along with the brine. Place the bag in a shallow dish in case it leaks, and refrigerate for 2 hours, rotating the trout every 30 minutes to make sure it remains submerged. Place the bag in a shallow dish in case of leakage.

**2.** Remove the trout from the brine and pat them dry with a paper towel.

**3.** Air-dry the brined trout in the refrigerator, uncovered, for 2 hours to allow the pellicle to form (see note on page 141 for more information).

## ON THE WOOD PELLET SMOKER-GRILL

**1.** Configure your wood pellet smoker-grill for indirect cooking. If your grill has cold-smoking capabilities, then configure your pellet smoker-grill for cold-smoking.

**2.** Preheat the grill to 180°F using alder pellets. A pit temperature of 180°F should result in a cold-smoke temperature of 70°F to 100°F in your smoker box, depending on the ambient temperature.

**3.** Cold-smoke the trout for 90 minutes.

**4.** After 90 minutes, transfer the cold-smoked boned trout to the wood pellet smoker-grill pit area and increase the wood pellet smoker-grill temperature to 225°F.

**5.** Continue cooking the trout until the internal temperature of the trout at the thickest part reaches 145°F.

**6.** Remove the trout from the grill and rest for 5 minutes before serving.

**NOTES**

Look for boned trout in the seafood department of your local grocery store, fish market, or better yet, catch your own and remove all the bones yourself.

Boned trout should be free of bones, but always take care when eating fish.

Cold-smoking occurs at temperatures between 70°F and 100°F.

# CHAPTER 6
# EXTRAS

# ARTISAN TAKE & BAKE PEPPERONI PIZZA

Delicious wood-fire-flavored pizza at home? Want to avoid cold, soggy delivered pizza? Then use your pellet smoker-grill for that crisp, piping hot, made-to-order, pepperoni or fully loaded combo pizza any time you want. When a craving for that pizza slice with your name on it rears its head and you don't have any pizza dough handy, then by all means don't hesitate: Get yourself a take-and-bake pizza from your favorite parlor or store, fire up the wood pellet smoker-grill, and satisfy those cravings. You'll be amazed at the results.

**SERVES: 4**

| **PREP TIME:** | **COOK TIME:** | **REST TIME:** |
|---|---|---|
| 5 minutes | 10 to 15 minutes | 5 minutes |

**RECOMMENDED PELLETS: Any**

take-and-bake pizza, such as Costco Kirkland Signature Take and Bake Artisan Pepperoni Pizza or toppings of your choice

## ON THE WOOD PELLET SMOKER-GRILL

**1.** Configure your wood pellet smoker-grill for indirect cooking and preheat to 400°F using any type of pellets.

**2.** If the pizza is refrigerated, remove it from the refrigerator 30 minutes prior to baking.

**3.** For a crispier crust, bake the pizza directly on the preheated conventional grill grates for 10 to 15 minutes, or until the cheese is bubbly and the crust is golden brown.

**4.** Using a pizza paddle, carefully remove the pizza from the grill and let stand for 5 minutes before slicing and serving.

# CRUSTY ARTISAN NO-KNEAD BREAD

This time-tested recipe creates chewy and moist yet crusty bread. This bread is laced with large air holes. The crisp, chewy crust is produced by the steam created inside a 5 or 6-quart enameled Dutch oven.

**SERVES: 4 to 6**

**PREP TIME:**
15 minutes (plus 12 to 18 hours rest time)

**COOK TIME:**
45 to 60 minutes

**REST TIME:**
15 minutes

**RECOMMENDED PELLETS: Any**

3 cups bread flour or all-purpose flour

1½ teaspoons kosher salt

½ teaspoon instant or rapid-rise yeast

1½ cups room-temperature water

## PREPPING FOR THE GRILL

**1.** In a large bowl, combine the flour, salt, and yeast.

**2.** Add the water and stir using a wooden spoon until dough has a sticky, shaggy texture. Cover the bowl with plastic wrap and let sit for 12 to 18 hours at room temperature.

**3.** After 12 or more hours the dough will be risen, dotted with bubbles, and sticky to the touch.

## ON THE WOOD PELLET SMOKER-GRILL

**1.** Configure your wood pellet smoker-grill for indirect cooking and preheat to 450°F using any pellets.

**2.** With floured hands, carefully remove the dough from the bowl and place on a lightly floured, clean, and dry surface. Gently form the dough into a ball and loosely cover with plastic wrap.

**3.** Preheat a 5 or 6-quart enameled Dutch oven for 30 minutes at 450°F while the dough is resting.

**4.** Remove the hot Dutch oven carefully from the grill and place the dough in the middle.

**5.** Cover and bake for 30 minutes.

**6.** Remove the cover and bake uncovered for an additional 15 to 30 minutes. The bread will be crusty, golden, and delicious when the internal temperature of the bread reaches 210°F.

**7.** Allow the bread to rest on a cooling rack for 15 minutes before serving.

**NOTES**

If you prefer to weigh your flour, 1 cup = 4.25 ounces.

# PIZZA DOUGH ROLLS

These pizza dough rolls are so easy to make, you'll wonder why you never made them before, but I guarantee you'll be making them often. Hot, fresh-off-the-grill, chewy, with a relatively thin crust, these rolls complement any meal.

**SERVES: 4 to 6**

**PREP TIME:**
15 minutes (plus 1½ to 2 hours rest time)

**COOK TIME:**
15 to 20 minutes

**RECOMMENDED PELLETS:** Any

2½ cups bread flour or all-purpose flour

1 teaspoon instant or rapid-rise yeast

1 teaspoon kosher salt

1 teaspoon sugar

1 cup warm water

1 tablespoon extra-virgin olive oil

## PREPPING FOR THE GRILL

**1.** In a large bowl, combine the flour, yeast, salt, and sugar.

**2.** Add the water and olive oil, and stir using a wooden spoon until the dough has a sticky, shaggy texture.

**3.** Knead the pizza dough lightly for 3 to 4 minutes using floured hands and cover with a flour-sack towel.

**4.** Let sit, covered, for 1 hour at room temperature. The dough should double in size.

**5.** On a clean, dry, lightly floured surface, divide the pizza dough into 8 equal portions. Form each portion into a roll shape using floured hands.

**6.** Cover a baking sheet or pizza pan with parchment paper, and place the rolls on the paper. Cover the rolls with a flour-sack towel.

**7.** Allow the rolls to rise again for 30 to 60 minutes, until they double in size.

## ON THE WOOD PELLET SMOKER-GRILL

**1.** Configure your wood pellet smoker-grill for indirect cooking and preheat to 400°F using any pellets.

**2.** Use a pair of scissors to score an "X" on top of each pizza dough roll.

**3.** Place the parchment-covered sheet or pan directly on the grill grates and bake for 15 to 20 minutes, until the rolls are golden brown and the internal temperature measured in the center of the rolls reaches 210°F.

**NOTES**

If you prefer to weigh your flour, 1 cup = 4.25 ounces.

# BANANA WALNUT BREAD

Irresistible banana walnut bread only requires a few easy steps to make. The results are so wonderful that you'll wish you made more than one loaf. The hardest part is waiting for the bananas to ripen enough to release the natural flavors and sugars needed for baking. Ripe bananas will look almost black when ready for use.

**YIELD: 1 loaf**

**PREP TIME:**
**15 minutes**

**COOK TIME:**
**60 to 75 minutes**

**REST TIME:**
**30 minutes**

**RECOMMENDED PELLETS: Any**

2½ cups all-purpose flour

1 cup mashed ripe bananas
(2 to 3 medium bananas)

1 cup finely chopped walnuts

1 cup sugar

¾ cup whole milk

1 large egg

3 tablespoons vegetable oil

3½ teaspoons baking powder

1 teaspoon salt

## PREPPING FOR THE GRILL

**1.** Grease and flour a loaf pan.

**2.** Combine all the ingredients in a large bowl.

**3.** Use a mixer at medium speed for 30 seconds to combine the ingredients, scraping the sides and bottom of the bowl while beating.

**4.** Pour the mixture into the loaf pan.

## ON THE WOOD PELLET SMOKER-GRILL

**1.** Configure your wood pellet smoker-grill for indirect cooking and preheat to 350° F using any pellets.

**2.** Bake for 60 to 75, minutes until a toothpick comes out clean when inserted in the center of the bread.

**3.** Remove the banana walnut bread loaf from the pan and allow it to cool on a cooling rack before slicing (unless you're like me and just can't wait!).

# CLASSIC APPLE PIE

What's more iconic than a slice of traditional apple pie with French vanilla ice cream? Once you've finished cooking your meal, bump up the wood pellet smoker-grill temperature to 425°F and bake a delicious apple pie for dessert. The best of both worlds—an entrée and a dessert.

**SERVES: 8**

**PREP TIME:**
30 minutes

**COOK TIME:**
45 to 60 minutes

**REST TIME:**
60 minutes

**RECOMMENDED PELLETS: Any**

6 cups thinly sliced peeled
Granny Smith apples (5 large)

¾ cup sugar

2 tablespoons all-purpose flour

1 tablespoon lemon juice

½ teaspoon ground cinnamon

¼ teaspoon salt

⅛ teaspoon ground nutmeg

1 box of 2 pie dough rounds,
or homemade pie dough

## PREPPING FOR THE GRILL

**1.** Combine the sliced apples, sugar, flour, lemon juice, cinnamon, salt, and nutmeg in a large bowl.

**2.** Firmly press one-half of the pie dough against the side and bottom of an ungreased 10-inch pie plate.

**3.** Pour the apple mixture into the crust-lined pie plate.

**4.** Cover the filling with the second pie crust. Using both hands, crimp the edges of the two crusts together to seal.

**5.** With a sharp knife, cut crosshatch slits in the top of the pie.

## ON THE WOOD PELLET SMOKER-GRILL

**1.** Configure your wood pellet smoker-grill for indirect cooking and preheat to 425°F using any pellets.

**2.** Bake the pie for 15 minutes. After 15 minutes, cover the edge of the crust with a wide strip of foil to prevent it from burning.

**3.** Bake for a total of 45 to 60 minutes, until the crust is golden brown.

**4.** Cool at least 1 hour on a cooling rack before serving.

**NOTES**

Serve with French vanilla ice cream, whipped cream, and/or slices of sharp cheddar cheese.

# PEACH BLUEBERRY COBBLER

The perfect ending to any meal is a fabulous cobbler with a scoop or two of French vanilla ice cream. The sweet flavor combinations of peaches and blueberries will delight any palate. This simple and easy recipe goes together in minutes, and best of all, you won't be heating up the kitchen during those hot summer days.

**SERVES: 4 to 6**

**PREP TIME:**
20 minutes

**COOK TIME:**
45 to 70 minutes

**REST TIME:**
5 minutes

**RECOMMENDED PELLETS: Any**

2 cups peeled sliced ripe peaches

1 cup fresh blueberries

1¼ cups white sugar, divided

½ cup (1 stick) salted butter, melted

1 cup all-purpose flour

2 teaspoons baking powder

½ teaspoon salt

1 cup whole milk

½ teaspoon pure vanilla extract

## PREPPING FOR THE GRILL

**1.** Combine the peaches, blueberries, and ¾ cup of sugar in a medium bowl, gently stirring until the fruit is fully coated, and set aside.

**2.** Melt the butter and set aside.

**3.** In a large bowl, whisk the flour, baking powder, salt, and remaining ½ cup sugar.

**4.** Add the milk, vanilla extract, and melted butter, and stir until just combined. Do not over-stir the batter; a few lumps are OK.

**5.** Pour the batter into a 2-quart ungreased baking dish.

**6.** Evenly pour the blueberries and peaches onto the batter (do not stir the cobbler).

## ON THE WOOD PELLET SMOKER-GRILL

**1.** Configure your wood pellet smoker-grill for indirect cooking and preheat to 375°F using any pellets.

**2.** Bake for 45 to 70 minutes, until the cobbler is golden brown and firm.

**3.** Rest for 5 minutes before serving hot.

**NOTES**

During baking, the batter rises to the top.

Serve hot with your choice of French vanilla ice cream and/or whipped cream.

Substitute your favorite berries and/or other fruit for the peaches and blueberries.

# CHAPTER 7
# BRINES AND RUBS

# BASIC POULTRY BRINE

This brine adds bright flavors and moisture to chicken and poultry recipes. Perfect for smoking, roasting, baking, and grilling. Feel free to mix and match different flavors to give your poultry a unique taste. I like to mix lemon and rosemary, soy sauce and garlic, Italian dressing and oregano—just to name a few. Have some fun and don't be afraid to experiment.

**MAKES: about 1 gallon**

**PREP TIME: 15 minutes**

1 gallon filtered water

½ cup white sugar

½ cup kosher or pickling salt

**OPTIONAL INGREDIENTS FOR FLAVOR UPGRADES:**

fresh lemon (halved, quartered, sliced, or grated zest)

2 bay leaves

¼ cup olive oil

¾ cup soy sauce

½ cup Italian salad dressing

2 to 4 garlic cloves, smashed

fresh or dried herbs and spices (thyme, rosemary, parsley, oregano, sage, cloves, etc.)

## DIRECTIONS

**1.** Place all the ingredients in a sealable plastic bag or brining container.

**2.** Mix until well blended.

**3.** Ensure that the meat is fully covered by the brine.

**4.** Store in the refrigerator.

| GUIDE FOR BRINING CHICKEN OR TURKEY | |
|---|---|
| Whole chicken (4 to 5 pounds) | 4 to 12 hours |
| Chicken pieces | 1 to 2 hours |
| Chicken breast | 1 hour |
| Whole turkey | 1 to 2 days |
| Turkey breast | 5 to 8 hours |
| Cornish game hen | 1 to 2 hours |

# PORK BRINE

Perfect for smoking, roasting, baking, and grilling, pork brine adds moisture and produces flavorful and succulent results. Brining is a simple procedure that chefs rarely share but is all the rage in professional kitchens. Depending on your preferences and tastes, I have offered a few optional ingredients below to add to your pork brine. Pairings are not cast in stone. Experiment and create your own favorites.

**MAKES: 1 gallon**

**PREP TIME: 15 minutes**

1 gallon filtered water

¾ cup brown sugar

¾ cup kosher salt

**OPTIONAL INGREDIENTS FOR FLAVOR UPGRADES:**

1 cup 100% apple juice

1 tablespoon mustard powder

2 garlic cloves, smashed

2 sprigs of thyme or rosemary

½ teaspoon black peppercorns

⅛ teaspoon red pepper flakes

## DIRECTIONS

**1.** Place all the ingredients in a sealable plastic bag or brining container.

**2.** Mix until well blended.

**3.** Ensure that the meat is fully covered by the brine.

**4.** Store in the refrigerator.

| GUIDE FOR BRINING PORK | |
|---|---|
| Whole pork loin | 2 to 4 days |
| Whole pork tenderloin | 6 to 12 hours |
| Pork chops (1 to 1½ inches thick) | 12 to 24 hours |

# BUTTERMILK BRINE

I designed this buttermilk brine for pork, but you'll find it works equally well with poultry.

**MAKES: about 1 quart**

**PREP TIME: 10 minutes**

1 quart cultured buttermilk

3 tablespoons extra-virgin olive oil

2 tablespoons crushed garlic

2 tablespoons Pete's Western Rub (page 169) or Fagundes Famous Seasoning

2 teaspoons black pepper

2 teaspoons onion powder

## DIRECTIONS

**1.** Place all the ingredients in a sealable plastic bag or brining container.

**2.** Mix until well blended.

**3.** Store in the refrigerator.

# SALMON AND TROUT BRINE

**MAKES: about 5 or 6 cups**

**PREP TIME: 15 minutes**

4 cups filtered water for salmon or 5 cups filtered water for trout

1 cup soy or teriyaki sauce

½ cup pickling or kosher salt

½ cup brown sugar

2 tablespoons garlic powder

2 tablespoons onion powder

1 teaspoon cayenne pepper (optional)

## DIRECTIONS

**1.** Combine all the ingredients together in two sealable 1-gallon bags or a 2-gallon food-grade plastic bag.

**2.** Store in the refrigerator.

# CAJUN SPICE RUB

Use this Cajun spice rub on your favorite cut of pork, poultry, or seafood.

**MAKES: about ⅓ cup**

**PREP TIME: 15 minutes**

1 tablespoon kosher salt

1 teaspoon black pepper

2 teaspoons garlic powder

1 teaspoon onion powder

2 teaspoons paprika

1 teaspoon oregano

1 teaspoon thyme

½ teaspoon cayenne pepper

½ teaspoon red pepper flakes (optional)

**For chicken, add the following:**

½ teaspoon rosemary

½ teaspoon sage

## DIRECTIONS

**1.** Place all the ingredients in a small bowl and mix until well blended.

**2.** Store in a cool area away from light in an airtight jar or sealable plastic bag.

# CREOLE SEAFOOD SEASONING

This seasoning provides layers of flavor profiles on fish of all kinds, like crawfish, crab, and gumbo recipes, just to name a few. Adjust quantities and ingredients to customize this seasoning to your specific needs and tastes. The source of the heat in Creole seasoning is cayenne pepper. I suggest you start at ½ tablespoon and adjust to your individual taste.

**MAKES: about 1 cup**

**PREP TIME: 15 minutes**

3 tablespoons smoked paprika

2½ tablespoons kosher salt

2 tablespoons black pepper

2 tablespoons pepper

1½ tablespoons onion powder

½ tablespoon cayenne pepper (or more as desired)

1 tablespoon dried thyme

1 tablespoon dried basil

1 tablespoon dried oregano

## DIRECTIONS

**1.** Place all the ingredients in a small bowl and mix until well blended.

**2.** Store in a cool area away from light in an airtight jar or sealable plastic bag.

# JAN'S ORIGINAL DRY RUB

Jan and Larry, known as KyNola on many barbecue/smoking/cooking forums, live in Kentucky, and in Larry's words, this is how his wife, Jan, developed her Original Dry Rub.

"My friend has a commercial barbecue restaurant and gave me some of his rub. He would not however, give me his recipe, so I put my wife on a mission to find something very similar on the Internet, which we would tweak to match his. Here is the result. It only has 14 ingredients and makes a large amount of rub."

Jan's Original Dry Rub was initially developed for poultry but is also excellent on pork. My son likes to use the rub on tri-tip roasts, with wonderful results. I have often said that Jan's recipe will make a brick taste fantastic! I salute Jan and everyone who has a palate to design, create, and perfect a rub, cure, brine, marinade, or sauce.

**MAKES: about 3 cups**

**PREP TIME: 25 minutes**

1¼ cups sugar

¼ cup Lawry's seasoned salt

¼ cup garlic salt

¼ cup plus 1½ teaspoons celery salt

¼ cup onion salt

½ cup paprika

3 tablespoons chili powder

2 tablespoons black pepper

1 tablespoon lemon pepper

2 teaspoons celery seed

2 teaspoons dried ground sage

1 teaspoon dried mustard

½ teaspoon dried ground thyme

½ teaspoon cayenne pepper

## DIRECTIONS

**1.** Place all the ingredients in a medium bowl and mix until well blended.

**2.** Store in a cool area away from light in an airtight jar or sealable plastic bag.

## PETE'S WESTERN RUB

Smoker Pete's Western Rub was created for beef but is a wonderful complement to poultry and excellent on vegetable dishes.

**MAKES: 1¼ cups**

**PREP TIME: 15 minutes**

1 cup kosher salt

6 tablespoons garlic powder

1 tablespoon onion powder

5 tablespoons dried oregano

3 tablespoons black pepper

3 tablespoons minced dried parsley

### DIRECTIONS

**1.** Place all the ingredients in a small bowl and mix until well blended.

**2.** Store in a cool area away from light in an airtight jar or sealable plastic bag.

## PORK DRY RUB

Use this all-purpose pork rub for your low-and-slow cooking, smoking, or roasting pork cuts, such as Boston butts, ribs, loins, tenderloins, and chops. Adjust the quantities and ingredients to customize this rub to your specific needs and tastes.

**MAKES: about ¾ cup**

**PREP TIME: 15 minutes**

¼ cup smoked paprika

¼ cup brown sugar

3 tablespoons kosher salt

2 tablespoons black pepper

2 tablespoons garlic powder

2 tablespoons onion powder

2 tablespoons chili powder

1 tablespoon cayenne pepper

1 teaspoon dried mustard

### DIRECTIONS

**1.** Place all the ingredients in a small bowl and mix until well blended.

**2.** Store in a cool area away from light in an airtight jar or sealable plastic bag.

# POULTRY SEASONING

Rather than buying a poultry seasoning, I recommend combining spices and herbs from your cabinet to make your own homemade seasoning.

**MAKES: about ¼ cup**

**PREP TIME: 15 minutes**

1 teaspoon ground sage

1 teaspoon ground thyme

1 teaspoon ground marjoram

1 teaspoon rosemary leaves

1 teaspoon celery salt

½ teaspoon smoked paprika

½ teaspoon onion powder

½ teaspoon ground nutmeg

¼ teaspoon black pepper

## DIRECTIONS

**1.** Place all the ingredients in a small bowl and mix until well blended.

**2.** Store in a cool area away from light in an airtight jar or sealable plastic bag.

# SEAFOOD SEASONING

Use this seafood seasoning for great flavors on fish of all kinds: shrimp, crab, oysters, and also on salads. Adjust quantities and ingredients to customize this seasoning to your specific needs and tastes.

**MAKES: about 1 cup**

**PREP TIME: 20 minutes**

5 tablespoons kosher salt

2 tablespoons dried mustard

2 tablespoons onion powder

1 tablespoon celery salt

1 tablespoon smoked paprika

2 teaspoons black pepper

1 teaspoon cayenne pepper

½ teaspoon ground cloves

½ teaspoon ground allspice

¼ teaspoon ground ginger

⅛ teaspoon ground cinnamon

## DIRECTIONS

**1.** Place all the ingredients in a small bowl and mix until well blended.

**2.** Store in a cool area away from light in an airtight jar or sealable plastic bag.

# TEXAS BARBECUE RUB

Texas barbecue rub naturally enhances beef, pork, poultry, vegetables, and wild game to highlight the true flavor associated with Texas-style barbecue. After being rubbed, meat can be refrigerated to allow the spices to marinate the meat, or it can be smoked or roasted right away.

**MAKES: about ½ cup**

**PREP TIME: 15 minutes**

2 tablespoons smoked paprika

1 tablespoon seasoned salt

1 tablespoon black pepper

1 tablespoon garlic powder

1 tablespoon onion powder

2 teaspoons chili powder

1 teaspoon cayenne pepper

1 teaspoon sugar

## DIRECTIONS

**1.** Place all the ingredients in a small bowl and mix until well blended.

**2.** Store in a cool area away from light in an airtight jar or sealable plastic bag.

# TEXAS-STYLE BRISKET RUB

Texas-style brisket dry rub should be rubbed 2 to 4 hours prior to smoking the brisket. Refrigerating the rubbed brisket overnight adds flavor by allowing the salt to penetrate the meat.

**MAKES: about 1 cup**

**PREP TIME: 15 minutes**

¼ cup smoked paprika

2 tablespoons kosher salt

2 tablespoons black pepper

2 tablespoons garlic powder

2 tablespoons onion powder

1 tablespoon cayenne pepper

2 teaspoons chipotle chili powder

2 teaspoons sugar

2 teaspoons ground cumin

## DIRECTIONS

**1.** Place all of the ingredients in a small bowl and mix until well blended.

**2.** Store in a cool area away from light in an airtight jar or sealable plastic bag.

# TUSCAN SEASONING

This blend of herbs and spices provides a warm Mediterranean flavor. Perfect for beef, chicken, seafood, and vegetables.

**MAKES: about 1 cup**

**PREP TIME: 15 minutes**

3 tablespoons kosher salt

3 tablespoons garlic powder

2 tablespoons onion powder

2 tablespoons rosemary leaves

2 tablespoons dried oregano

1 tablespoon dried basil

1 tablespoon black pepper

2 teaspoons crushed red pepper

## DIRECTIONS

**1.** Place all the ingredients in a small bowl and mix until well blended.

**2.** Store in a cool area away from light in an airtight jar or sealable plastic bag.

# CONVERSIONS

## VOLUME CONVERSIONS

| U.S. | U.S. EQUIVALENT | METRIC |
|---|---|---|
| 1 tablespoon (3 teaspoons) | ½ fluid ounce | 15 milliliters |
| ¼ cup | 2 fluid ounces | 60 milliliters |
| ⅓ cup | 3 fluid ounces | 90 milliliters |
| ½ cup | 4 fluid ounces | 120 milliliters |
| ⅔ cup | 5 fluid ounces | 150 milliliters |
| ¾ cup | 6 fluid ounces | 180 milliliters |
| 1 cup | 8 fluid ounces | 240 milliliters |
| 2 cups | 16 fluid ounces | 480 milliliters |

## WEIGHT CONVERSIONS

| U.S. | METRIC |
|---|---|
| ½ ounce | 15 grams |
| 1 ounce | 30 grams |
| 2 ounces | 60 grams |
| ¼ pound | 115 grams |
| ⅓ pound | 150 grams |
| ½ pound | 225 grams |
| ¾ pound | 350 grams |
| 1 pound | 450 grams |

# TEMPERATURE CONVERSIONS

| FAHRENHEIT (°F) | CELSIUS (°C) |
|---|---|
| 70°F | 20°C |
| 100°F | 40°C |
| 120°F | 50°C |
| 130°F | 55°C |
| 140°F | 60°C |
| 150°F | 65°C |
| 160°F | 70°C |
| 170°F | 75°C |
| 180°F | 80°C |
| 190°F | 90°C |
| 200°F | 95°C |
| 220°F | 105°C |
| 240°F | 115°C |
| 260°F | 125°C |
| 280°F | 140°C |
| 300°F | 150°C |
| 325°F | 165°C |
| 350°F | 175°C |
| 375°F | 190°C |
| 400°F | 200°C |
| 425°F | 220°C |
| 450°F | 230°C |

# COOKING TIMES

| | RARE | MEDIUM RARE | MEDIUM | MEDIUM WELL | WELL | USDA MINIMUM |
|---|---|---|---|---|---|---|
| **RED MEAT: BEEF AND LAMB** | | | | | | |
| Brisket | | | | | 200–205°F | |
| Chuck Short Ribs | | | | | 195–205°F | |
| Ground Meats | | | | | 160°F | 160°F |
| Leg of Lamb | 125°F | 130°F | 135–140°F | 145°F | 150°F | 145°F |
| New York Strip Roast | 125°F | 130°F | 140°F | 150°F | 160°F | 145°F |
| Rack of Lamb | 120–125°F | 130–135°F | 140–145°F | 150–155°F | 160°F | 145°F |
| Steaks (1½-inch thick) | 125°F | 130°F | 140°F | 150°F | 160°F | 145°F |
| Tri-Tip Roasts | 125°F | 130°F | 140°F | 150°F | 160°F | 145°F |
| **PORK** | | | | | | |
| Boston/Pork Butt | | | | | 200–205°F | |
| Ground Pork | | | | | 160°F | 160°F |
| Loin Chops | | | 145–150°F | | | 145°F |
| Loin Roast | | | 145–150°F | | | 145°F |
| Rack of Pork | | | 145–150°F | | | 145°F |
| Ready-to-Cook Ham | | | | | 160°F | 160°F |
| Ready-to-Eat Ham | | | | | 140°F | 140°F |
| Ribs | | | | | 185–190°F | |
| Sirloin Tip Roast | | | 145–150°F | | | 145°F |
| Tenderloin Roast | | | 145–150°F | | | 145°F |

| | RARE | MEDIUM RARE | MEDIUM | MEDIUM WELL | WELL | USDA MINIMUM |
|---|---|---|---|---|---|---|
| **POULTRY** | | | | | | |
| Dark Meat | | | | | 180°F | 165°F |
| Ground Poultry | | | | | 165°F | 165°F |
| White Meat | | | | | 170°F | 165°F |
| **SEAFOOD** | | | | | | |
| Salmon | | | | 140°F | 145°F | 145°F |
| Pacific Rockfish | | | | 140°F | 145°F | 145°F |
| Tilapia | | | | 140°F | 145°F | 145°F |
| Smoked Tuna | | | | | 145°F | 145°F |
| Smoked Salmon | | | | | 145°F | 145°F |
| Smoked Trout | | | | | 145°F | 145°F |
| Fish and Shellfish | | | | | 145°F | 145°F |

# INDEX

# ACKNOWLEDGMENTS

A ton of appreciation to everyone that has inspired me over the years to pursue my love for cooking. What started as a job as a short order cook at age 16 has since become my full-blown hobby and passion at age 66. Over the years I've received wonderful support and feedback from my family, friends, my extended family on various cooking forums, and the fans of my blog. My wife, Karen, has been my biggest inspiration and fan always, providing me with constructive reviews of my cooks. Karen played the biggest part in my recipe development for this cookbook by tasting the good, the bad, and the ugly!

I want to extend a special thanks to the Tucker family and staff at MAK Grills for all their support over the years.

# ABOUT THE AUTHOR

**Peter Jautaikis** is the barbecue pitmaster of the blog *Smokin' Pete's BBQ* (www.smokinpetebbq.com). Pete's recipes and photographs are featured on various forums and barbecue wood pellet and smoker-grill manufacturer websites. Peter has two sons and five grandchildren. He lives in Ripon, California, with his wife of 43 years.

When Peter is not in the backyard grilling, he and his wife are traveling the country in their RV—but he never leaves home without his portable Green Mountain Davy Crockett grill.

# Other Ulysses Press Books

Exclusively Kamado

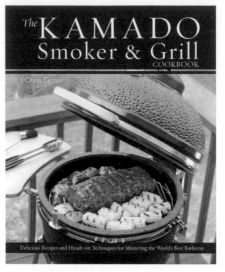

The Kamado Smoker & Grill
Cookbook

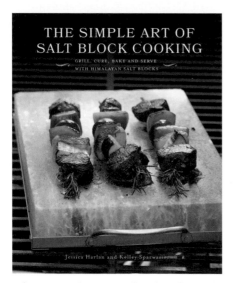

The Simple Art of Salt Block
Cooking

Smoke It Like a Pit Master
with Your Electric Smoker

To order these books call 800-377-2542 or 510-601-8301, fax 510-601-8307, e-mail ulysses@ulyssespress.com, or write to Ulysses Press, P.O. Box 3440, Berkeley, CA 94703. All retail orders are shipped free of charge. California residents must include sales tax. Allow two to three weeks for delivery.